CHRISTOS

The Religion of the Future

by

WILLIAM KINGSLAND

THE BOOK TREE
San Diego, California

Originally published
1929
by John M. Watkins
London

ISBN 978-1-58509-325-0

Cover layout and design
by Toni Villalas

Published by
The Book Tree
P.O. Box 16476
San Diego, CA 92176
www.thebooktree.com

CONTENTS

Foreword

When one examines the path of history it becomes clear that mankind is learning and evolving. Although we are still animals in a biological sense, what separates us from them is the evolution of the mind. According to the author, this evolution moves through three stages: the physical, the mental, and then the spiritual. Most of us are still in the mental stage. Our religions are a reflection of this shortcoming, but as we become more spiritually aware, our religions will have to change. This is already starting to happen, especially with Christianity. Kingsland predicted this back in 1929, when this book was first published. Regarding Christianity he said, "There are two courses open to it: either to strip itself of its pagan accretions and get back to the simple religion of Jesus, or to recognize the allegorical nature of its present literalised Scriptures, and to understand and teach the real and original *Gnosis* from which these sprang: the real inner spiritual meaning as known to the Initiates who formulated them."

That is what this book is about. Kingsland shows that certain outdated beliefs and dogmas from a far less enlightened time have been carried over into the present and are no longer valid in light of our modern knowledge. As a result, we are rediscovering Gnosis as a deeper, more meaningful answer. Much about Gnosis is covered, but Kingsland makes it clear that he does not refer to the ancient Hellenistic Gnosticism with the term. It instead indicates a supreme degree of knowledge—something we had found briefly in the past, and are becoming ready to embrace, more fully, in the future.

Paul Tice

PREFACE

I do but echo in this little work the views of thousands of well-informed thinkers in the Western World at the present time.

On the other hand, the beliefs which are here perhaps somewhat strongly represented as being primitive and obsolete, are still those of many millions; and I recognise that they must remain so for many a long day yet to come. They are still the authoritative teachings of the Roman and Anglican Churches, as well as the 'faith' of that wonderful organisation, the Salvation Army, for whose work I have a profound admiration. They are also more or less the tenets of innumerable other Christian sects.

As for the Eastern World, it is scarcely necessary to say that Christianity has hardly touched the religious beliefs of India, China, or Japan, not to mention other lesser countries. The total adherents of the Eastern religions far exceeds that of the whole population of the nations which are supposed to be 'Christian', but not one-tenth of whose inhabitants can really be designated as such.

Those who know anything at all of these Eastern religions can hardly be surprised that 'Christianity' should have made so little headway in the East; not merely because of the inherent merits of these religions, and their greater adaptation to the mentality of the Eastern peoples, but perhaps even more so because of the discrepancy between Christian doctrines and their exemplification in the 'Christian' nations.

When all is said and done, formal religions are the outcome of the *mentality* of the race, the community, and the age in which they arise. We must always make allowances for this, and not expect any one form to be universally acceptable, or even understandable.

For the purpose of this work I am defining Religion as *the effort of the individual to realise his innate spiritual nature and powers.* This is what I understand Religion to be *at root.* It applies to Mankind as a whole, to the Race as well as to the Individual. Anything that ministers to this must be considered to be an accessory to Religion, though not Religion itself. The one is only too often mistaken for the other.

We may note, however, that the effort may

be, in the first instance, a blind unconscious "feeling after God"; indeed, it would appear that such must necessarily have been the commencement of religion with primitive races. It implies a *relation* to some Deity, and hence the innumerable gods and conceptions of 'God' invented by man. But in the higher stages the universal testimony of the mystics is to the experience of *unification*. Moreover, the history of religious experience shows us many strange expressions of this inner impulse.[1]

I have an equal love and admiration for the devotee of each and every religion who endeavours to *practise* what he professes to believe, and to live the life indicated by the original founder or founders of that particular religion. In respect of ethics, however, there is little room for choice. All religions worthy of the name must necessarily teach the fundamental principles of right conduct; but ethics alone is not religion.

As for beliefs and creeds, these are merely the outer garments in which the religionist dresses up according to the conventions of his time and his community. A good Christian

[1] See in particular *The Varieties of Religious Experience*, by Wm. James.

would have made an equally good Buddhist if he had happened to have been born in a Buddhist community. The mischief is that these garments are not merely commonly assumed to be 'the real thing', but are largely worn for mere convention and respectability; and only too often, indeed, to mask insincerity and hypocrisy, and as a cloak for unrighteousness.

I hold that whilst not judging the individual for his beliefs, or even for his actions, we have every right—and might, indeed, consider it to be our bounden duty—to denounce and oppose with all our might both beliefs and actions which are intrinsically evil, or which give rise to evil in the form of superstitious practices and bigoted intolerance and persecution. We have every right to denounce both beliefs and systems which have been, and are, a fruitful cause of these. We have in this respect quite clearly the example of the founder of Christianity.

What I have here endeavoured to do, merely in outline, is to show that certain modern beliefs, dogmas, and creeds, which have been carried over and have survived from a far less enlightened age or period, can no longer be valid in the light of our modern knowledge. There is, of course, nothing new in this ; many writers are doing it to-day.

But, further than that, I shall hope to indicate that even in the remotest past there was already a deeper knowledge, a real *Gnôsis* which we are in fact only now beginning to recover.[1]

It is that ancient *Gnôsis* which must be the Religion of the Future ; for, as I shall hope to show to some extent, all our scientific discoveries and our modern philosophical thinking tends to confirmation and re-statement of it.

RYDE, I.W. W. K.
September, 1929.

[1] In this work I do not use the term *Gnôsis* with any special reference to the Hellenistic *Gnosticism*, but simply as indicating a supreme degree of knowledge, and more particularly in mystical religion.

CHRISTOS

The Religion of the Future

Religions and Religion

Will there be any religions at all in the future?

Note that I say religions, not Religion.

But, in the first place, shall we speak of the more immediate future—say one hundred, or perhaps one thousand years hence—or shall we speak of, say, one million years?

I will leave it to my readers to decide as I proceed which of these periods is the most applicable to the principles I shall endeavour to elucidate.

We may note here, however, that one million years is not much more than a day—possibly not even that—in the whole history of the Race,[1] and there is every indication that Humanity as a whole is still very young. Certainly in the matter of religion the great majority have not as yet developed any real appreciation of their spiritual nature and

[1] See page 35, *The Age of the Earth*

faculties, nor have they even attained to the mental capacity of which man is clearly capable, as seen by the attainments of a few. Were it otherwise, the world would be a very different place from what it is to-day. In matters of religion the great majority still "speak as a child, feel as a child, and think as a child."

Mankind as a whole has been in the past, and is to-day, superstitious rather than religious. Or perhaps we had better say that though religion itself, as an effort of the individual to realise his relation to the superphysical or 'spiritual' world, is both Man's highest effort and most deeply rooted instinct, yet it has hitherto, in his profound ignorance of the laws and nature of the physical world —let alone the superphysical—taken the form of superstition and supernaturalism rather than a clear realisation of his own inherent spiritual nature and powers.

Yet over and over again these have been presented to him, back from the remotest time of which we have any literary records; but always and ever the great majority have materialised and debased the pure teachings.

Religion, as the effort of Man to realise his spiritual nature and faculties, lies in the natural line of his evolution as a further stage beyond the development of his mind or intellect. He has struggled from the merely animal—not to go any further back—to what we at present call the human; though precisely when he first became *homo sapiens* it is impossible to say. He is still an animal physiologically, and indeed even very much so mentally, though his great distinction from the animal is in the evolution of Mind.

But, at all events for some millenniums, he has reached forward to something still higher. The best and the wisest and the noblest of the Race have done so in no uncertain manner from the earliest times of which we have any knowledge in script or monument, and undoubtedly also ages before that. But the great bulk of the Race lag behind these exemplars; indeed they tail off, even to-day, to something little better than a somewhat more intelligent animal. Thus we have in the line of Man's *ascent* or evolution—not '*descent*' —first the physical, then the mental, then the spiritual. But, as I shall show later on, this *ascent* is simply his *return* to his Source; the completion of the great cycle of Cosmic Man in his outgoing or 'fall'—into physical life —and his return or 'redemption': his 'resurrection' from his present loss of consciousness of his spiritual nature; represented in the New Testament as 'sleep' and 'death'. We are able to trace in biology and history the stages of Man's *ascent*, but we know little or nothing of the stages of the *descent*, save as these are given to us in allegory and in parable, as for example in *Genesis* and in the parable of the prodigal son.

Man becomes at first vaguely conscious of a *soul*, of a part of his being which is related to a, or *The*, great underlying *Power* which IS the Universe in which he lives and moves and has his being. This reaching out to an underlying unseen REALITY is Religion—whether as science, as philosophy, or as what more generally goes by the name of religion in its institutional forms.

Religion, however, is not a mere matter of individual salvation. "The whole creation groaneth and travaileth in pain together until now." It is a *cosmic* process, from which the individual can in no wise separate himself. It is the great effort of "all creation" to return to its Source after the outgoing cycle. "I will arise and go to my Father." And he who does not recognise the stages by which in the vast cycle of evolution he has reached his present development with the rest of humanity, and who has no response in his heart for "the world's great pain"—not for his fellow man only, but for all the 'lower Kingdoms' also—has still much to learn and far to go.

Answering then our first question with a seeming paradox, we might say that though possibly there may be no *institutional* religions in the future such as we have with us to-day, yet Man will be incomparably more religious then than now.

Religions, in so far as they are institutional —with a definite set of beliefs, creeds, dogmas, and ritual—are not Religion, though they are what is commonly understood by the term. They are, indeed, mostly departures from Religion: perversions of originally pure spiritual teachings. They quickly abandon the simplicity and intention of their founders, and become involved in endless doctrinal disputes. They quickly lose their spiritual character, and become hardened, materialised, literalised and secularised. They become worldly institutions, with exclusive, individualistic, and proselytising aims. They become the slayers of truth rather than its exponents and exemplars.

For the very reason that religion is Man's

highest effort and deepest instinct, it is potent for the greatest evils as well as for the highest good. It is the origin and nourisher of the grossest superstitions and the most cruel practices, as well as of the sublimest ideals and the most saintly lives. It has drenched the world in blood, and claimed a holocaust of tortured victims. Fire and sword and persecution, the rack and the stake, are associated even with what claims to be the supreme religion of Love and Peace. In its institutional and hierarchical forms it has fostered the continuance of superstition and ignorance for the benefit of shameless priest-craft; and has served as a cloak, and even as an excuse, for the grossest sensualism. Even stranger still, perhaps, thousands of devotees have tortured themselves for the sake of their religious convictions. Whether Indian fakir or Christian ascetic, whether the idea centres on the conception of the will of an Idol or that of the Christian God, the motive and the psychology is the same. At root the individual is trying to find his own soul; to realise *himself*.

All these things have been, and are to-day, associated with the *name* of religion; but are they in any sense the legitimate products of

Religion itself ? They are certainly the products of *institutional* religion, of formulated creeds; and we might well decide that institutional religion as the formulator of creeds has ever been the perverter of religion rather than its exponent, its exemplar, and its preserver.

Our question is, then, not as to whether religion as such will survive. There can be no question as to that, for the instinct in Man to reach out to the Root and Source of his being must necessarily grow stronger with every increase in his knowledge and capacity for fathoming the depths of the Universe around him, and the latent powers in his own nature which he feels himself capable of developing in ever greater and greater degree. Therefore would I account all genuine scientific investigation as a necessary part of religion. The distinction between the religious and the secular which has hitherto been made has been for the most part purely artificial. Religions have made themselves the great exception, even from reason itself. A supposed revelation, and dogmas associated therewith, have endeavoured to take the place of rational beliefs. Yet clearly any revelation can only be as is the capacity to receive; and when the individual is capable of receiving, is capable of mental perception, the supposed secret is as open to him as is the physical object when the eye is adapted to see it.

Man's consciousness will inevitably expand. New faculties—or rather faculties now latent, but the possibilities of which are in evidence in abnormal individuals—will come into play, and ever and always his evolution must bring him nearer and nearer to a realisation of his own inherent spiritual nature and powers.

Religion thus viewed is simply the *natural* process of Man's evolution, and not any *super*-natural ordinance of the God or Gods he has himself invented in his childish days.

Our question is as to whether institutional religion, based for the most part on primitive conceptions of a *supernatural* character, can survive the progress of our scientific knowledge, and the readjustment of our views as to the nature of the universe and of Man himself which must inevitably result therefrom and be common property through the facilities for the spread of knowledge which our modern civilisation provides.

Already we hear on every side of the waning influence of institutional Christianity. If that finally decays—as indeed would appear to be inevitable in the course of time—what will replace it? Will some new religion take its place, or will it reform itself out of all recognition of its present characteristics?

There are two courses open to it: either to strip itself of its pagan accretions and get back to the simple religion of Jesus, or to recognise the allegorical nature of its present literalised Scriptures, and understand and teach the real and original *Gnôsis* from which these sprang: the real inner spiritual meaning as known to the Initiates who formulated them. I shall endeavour later on to show to some extent how these allegories can be brought into line with our knowledge in other departments of our human experience.

But it will be harder for the Church thus to abandon its present ground than for a rich man to enter into the kingdom of heaven; for the reformers will have to reckon not merely with a deeply rooted popular tradition, but also with a great institutional hierarchy, loath to depart from the sumptuous edifice which shelters and enriches it.

The Church of England would disestablish itself to-morrow were it not for the dread word *disendowment*. Has it then not faith enough to believe that if it seeks *first* the

Kingdom of God and His righteousness, all these things will be added unto it?

With the passing of superstition and supernaturalism, will religion once and for all throw off its evil association—perhaps a necessary evil in the meanwhile—with a priestly hierarchy of which these are the main support?

Our question may even take the form as to whether any concept of a *personal* God can survive. The question of Deity is a fundamental one, and we must examine it somewhat more in detail.

The Concept of a Personal God

The concept of a personal Deity has already gone with all philosophical thinkers in the West; indeed, as the *Upanishads* and other Eastern literature shows us, it had gone ages ago with the deepest thinkers in the East. Its place is taken to-day in philosophy by the concept of the *Absolute,* or *Reality*—a fundamental Reality which IS the Universe. This one fundamental eternal Reality can be described as a PRINCIPLE, but never as a Person.

It may seem strange to many minds to have religion without a personal God; but that already obtains in the Eastern religious philosophies, more particularly in the Vedânta and in Buddhism, and it is these impersonal religions which are the most free from the rancours, strifes, and persecutions which accompany more or less all religions in proportion as they degenerate into dogmas and formulas. It would appear, indeed, in the general history of religion, that in proportion as the personality of the Deity is accentuated, so are the evils of the institutional forms.

And in proportion as the impersonal nature of THAT which IS the Universe is recognised, so do these evils vanish, and freedom of thought and toleration take their place.

All theological propositions about 'God' are found on analysis to be self-contradictory, but it is essential to remember that every teacher has to adapt his teaching to the understanding of his hearers, and the general notions of the time and the community to which he belongs. The teachings of Jesus had to be adapted to the crude Jewish conceptions of a personal God, who required above all things to be propitiated and worshipped ; and it would appear that his presentation of a heavenly *Father* was the most reformative one that his hearers were capable of understanding. Gautama Buddha, on the other hand, had to deal with minds of quite another order, and accordingly we find that he refused to personify or in any way define the Absolute. When questioned as to the nature of this Absolute Principle he was silent. So also the Upanishads. *Neti, neti,* not this, not that, is the answer to all attempts to give attributes to THAT. But this negation is really the explicit of a much larger affirmation. Let us understand clearly that the primitive mind requires a *Gospel* (*lit.* Good News): something which, adapted to the mental capacity of the hearers, would appear to console for the evils and trials of life. Yet what may be a Gospel for one man, or one community, is very far from being so for others. Whatever it may have been for the ignorance of that part of the world in which the Christian theology was formulated, the statement that one had "risen from the dead, and become the first-fruits of them that slept", could be no 'Gospel' to those in possession of the ancient Wisdom Religion of the East: of India, Chaldea, Egypt, or the Gnostics and Initiates of Greece.

What sort of 'Gospel' could it have been to Plato or Socrates, not to mention Confucius, Lâo Tsze, Guatama Buddha, Shankara Âchârya, or innumerable others who lived and wrote centuries B.C.? What sort of a 'Gospel' can it be to us if taken in its crude materialised form? The dead do not 'sleep', awaiting the resurrection of their physical bodies. The resurrection of the *physical* body of Jesus cannot be accepted as a historical fact; or even if it is, it has by no means the significance attached to it as "the first-fruits of them that slept". We might indeed say that Christian theology, far from being a 'Gospel', has done more than anything else to put the fear of death and Hell into the hearts of untold millions. Some of the early Church Fathers knew better, but their teaching has been ignored. How, for example, could this 'Gospel' apply to the teaching of Origen contained in the following passage.

> "The present inequalities of circumstances and character are thus not wholly explicable within the sphere of the present life. But this world is not the only world. Every soul has existed from the beginning; it has therefore passed through some worlds already, and will pass through others before it reaches the final consummation. It comes into this world strengthened by the victories or weakened by the defeats of its previous life. Its place in this world as a vessel appointed to honour or dishonour is determined by its previous merits or demerits. Its work in this world determines its place in the world which is to follow this."

But when we understand the *spiritual* meaning of "resurrection from the dead"; when we understand that it is not *physical* death that is referred to at all, but the deadness of Man's spiritual nature until his Christ Principle has risen again *in him*—it having been dead and buried by his "descent into matter" ; whereby hangs also the meaning of the 'Fall'—we are no longer in conflict with a wider and deeper knowledge. There are a great many references in the New Testament to the resurrection from the dead which have this spiritual meaning, though they are commonly taken as if they referred to a physical death and resurrection. Both sleep and death are associated with the spiritual condition of the *living* in many passages which might be called to mind.

> "Now it is high time for you to awaken out of sleep" (Rom. xv. 11).
>
> "If by any means I may attain to the resurrection from the dead" (Phil. iii. 11).

We are far from despising the simple childlike faith in a heavenly Father who sees and knows every thought and action of every single individual, and who personally adjusts the daily supply and the daily tasks and trials to the needs of the individual—at least for those who pray to him for help and guidance. Even as in the time of Jesus and Paul, there are still primitive minds in these matters who can only be fed with milk, not with strong meat, with parables, not with metaphysics. It is really astonishing, however, and even pathetic, how many intelligent people to-day are as yet merely primitive children in matters of religion. The psychology of religious beliefs is no different from the psychology of other beliefs; and all beliefs are largely a matter of psychology and not of reason. We meet every day with innumerable cases of auto-suggestion of the most absurd character. By auto-suggestion, continual meditation on the Passion of the Cross, St. John of the Cross and other Christian mystics produced actual stigmata marks on their hands. That proved nothing beyond the power of auto-suggestion. The effect would have been the same even were the Crucifixion only an allegory and not an historical event, but of course the *belief* in its historicity must be there. The sectarian religionist moves within the narrow circle of his own mind and that of the community to which he belongs. He has neither the will nor the capacity to inquire into other modes of thought, or other religions. Believing that he already has the truth, the whole truth, and nothing but the truth—and indeed that it would be a sin to question the basis of his beliefs—he goes on his way rejoicing, and perhaps pitying, even if not looking askance at those who differ from him.

The close and intimate experience of divine guidance and communion which is so real to many devotees, saints, and mystics, comes from the depths of one's own being, which is, and never can be other than *one with* the absolute, the ONE LIFE, however much the outer man, the conventional 'self,' the ever-changing phenomenal personality, may appear to be separated therefrom, and therefore refers this experience to an external personal God.

Man creates his own Gods and his own Devils; but we clearly see that in all ages there have been those who have transcended the crude popular notions which attach to these, and which for the most part are based on a simple realism which takes the objective world to be exactly what it seems.

But religious beliefs based on crude realism cannot possibly survive the present spread of knowledge. That is not to say that Religion itself will be destroyed. Something much more *real*, much more fundamental will certainly take the place of the present crudities. In so far as every advance of knowledge brings us nearer to *Reality*—nearer in our concepts, that is to say—it brings us nearer to a clear apprehension of the real nature of the problems of our life and consciousness; and the more it does that, the more we apprehend that the *appearance* of things—as also our consciousness of time and space—are veils which hide from us rather than disclose the One Eternal Reality. They can only be disclosures of Reality in proportion as we penetrate beneath their appearances as time and space phenomena, and learn to recognise that underlying REALITY which *endures*.

If I am asked to define Reality, I shall say that Reality is that which *endures*. It is that which changes not amidst all change; and it must be not merely the unchanging Reality underlying the objective world but the subjective also. To find it, the man must penetrate to the depths of his own being. He must find that in himself which *endures*; that which is independent of the phenomenal world; that deeper *Self* which has never not been, nor can ever cease to be. He must find his true *Self*, and can only do so as he lets go of the phenomenal changing *personality* to which at present he clings so desperately, and is even much afraid lest it should not be 'saved'. And therein lies the paradox that whosoever would save his life must lose it. The finding of the true Self is a continual negation, a perpetual 'loss' of the phenomenal self.

So long as the individual thinks himself separate from the underlying *Reality*—which he must always do so long as he conceives of it as a *personal* God—he must remain in the outer courts of the Temple, and worship afar off. But when he has realised his oneness with the One Imperishable REALITY there is no longer room for the personal Gods which he formerly worshipped.

Superstition and Supernaturalism

I have several times used the words *superstition* and *supernaturalism.* They are so closely associated with the subject of religion, and are so often used in a loose manner, that it will be necessary at this point to examine their meaning and implications more definitely.

The two terms are clearly allied, for superstition implies the supernatural. A Dictionary definition of superstition is as follows:

> "Belief or a specific form of belief in which ignorant and abnormal religious feeling is shown, as by venerating things that deserve no veneration, or by attaching undue importance to forms and observances in themselves; also any practice founded on such beliefs."

A secondary meaning is given as:

> "Credulity regarding the supernatural." [1]

The first of these definitions is exceedingly unsatisfactory, since it leaves the question

[1] Standard Dictionary.

quite open as to what things are or are not deserving of veneration. To the Protestant the Mass and the veneration of the Virgin are superstitions, but they are not so for the Roman Catholic.

The second definition immediately raises the question as to what is the supernatural. Where does 'Nature' end and the *super*-natural begin? Apart from this question, the word carries its own meaning. There is a general theological meaning, however, attached to the term which recognises that God the Creator is beyond 'Nature,' and that therefore any direct action attributed to Him is a supernatural act.

Now as regards the term 'Nature', there is no doubt that in the old sense of the word it simply meant the physical world of matter and force; or more broadly it meant everything that could be seen and accounted for within the limits of what was known as 'natural law'. Hence the unseen and the apparently unaccountable was relegated to the field of operation of the supernatural. It was peopled with beings—or with a Being: the theological God—who could *interfere* with the course of Nature, and so produce a 'miracle'.

But nothing can be more evident than that the supposed boundary line between the natural and the supernatural is a purely artificial one, dependent merely on our knowledge for the time being—or perhaps we should rather say our ignorance—of the laws of Nature. In bygone times there was no difficulty in conceiving of the supernatural as being just beyond the limits of the seen and known world. It was entered at death. It was the 'spirit world', and is so to-day with very large numbers of people. But our modern scientific knowledge has not merely disposed of innumerable 'superstitions' which formerly attached to this super-physical region but it has also raised the much larger question as to whether there is any line of demarcation whatsoever between the natural and the supernatural; whether in fact the whole universe, seen or unseen, is not one great *natural* Whole, governed by law and order from centre to circumference or rather from the innermost to the outermost, though these terms also are merely arbitrary ones of our normal perceptions. Perhaps it would be better to say that all is *natural* from Matter to Spirit, and to conceive of these as the two contrasted poles of one unitary Reality. The polarity is due to the limitations of the mind or intellect, and not to anything intrinsic in the nature of the Reality itself—as, indeed, modern philosophers are now beginning clearly to understand.

Last century the reaction from the supernaturalism and superstition of the previous centuries, brought about by our brilliant scientific discoveries, led to the other extreme, and *materialism* became associated with the concepts of a great many scientific men. Mind and consciousness were considered to be simply the products or 'epiphenomena' of matter and force.

But there were deeper thinkers even among the scientists, who saw that such a generalisation was very far from being legitimate. Thomas Henry Huxley, though he has commonly been accounted a materialist, protested most strongly against the materialistic doctrine. In *Evolution and Ethics* he writes as follows:

"It seems to me pretty plain that there is a third thing in the universe, to wit, consciousness, which, in the hardness of my heart or head, I cannot see to be matter, or force, or any conceivable modification of either, however intimately the manifestations of the phenomena of consciousness may be connected with the phenomena known as matter and force. . . . Take the simplest possible example, the feeling of redness. Physical science tells us that it commonly arises as a consequence of molecular changes propagated from the eye to a certain part of the substance of the brain, when vibrations of the luminiferous ether of a certain character fall upon the retina. Let us suppose the process of physical analysis pushed so far that one could view the last link of this chain of molecules, watch their movements as if they were billiard balls, weigh them, measure them, and know all that is physically knowable about them. Well, even in that case, we should be just as far from being able to include the resulting phenomenon of consciousness, the feeling of redness, within the bounds of physical science, as we are at present. It would remain as unlike the phenomena we know under the names of matter and motion as it is now. If there is any plain truth upon which I have made it my business to insist over and over again it is this."

And now we have Professor Eddington [1] coming forward and reinforcing this view with all the weight of our most recent science based on the principles of relativity and the quantum. Physical science is shown to be a closed region of " pointer readings "—namely, the numerical indications of our physical instruments of measurement—which can be dealt

[1] *The Nature of the Physical World.*

with mathematically, but which cannot possibly enter the super-physical region of mind and consciousness. These latter are direct knowledge, whereas the very existence of 'matter' is only an inference. Instead of Huxley's billiard-ball atoms[1] we are now presented with electrons and protons. Somewhere and somehow in the physical brain the vibrations of these become translated into sensations which are totally unlike anything that science can formulate about them—as for example, the sensation of colour. At this point, in fact, we cannot say whether it is an external world in which 'matter' has a reality of its own, or whether that world is not a construct of mind itself.

The wider and deeper scientific knowledge which this present century has brought us, and more particularly the discovery of the break-up and constitution of physical matter, at the same time that it has vastly deepened our concepts of 'Nature', has entirely disposed of the nineteenth-century materialism.

But there is another aspect of this question which we must not overlook. Without referring back to any super-natural beings or

[1] The common conception of an atom during the last century was that of an elastic particle, like a billiard-ball "only more so".

Being, we see clearly that we ourselves exercise supernatural powers in so far as we are able to direct and control the laws which we recognise as conditioning the external world of what we call 'Nature'. I must surely be *super—i.e.*, above, over, beyond—anything that I can control. I can set one law against the other. I can inhibit a phenomenon which would otherwise take place 'naturally' by bringing into operation a counter law. We can do things to-day by our knowledge of natural law which our forefathers would have roundly declared to be impossible save by a 'miracle'. Who shall say what we may or may not be able to do to-morrow? To-day, in ignorance of the deeper laws of nature, more particularly of the action of mind upon matter, a great many 'superstitious' religionists still regard certain things as 'miracles', and attribute them to the direct action of a personal God—and in some cases to a personal Devil.

Mind, in so far as it can control the external laws of matter and force, and direct them for its own purposes, is clearly superior to them; but at the same time we cannot doubt that there are laws which determine the action of mind upon matter. If we knew more about these laws, we should doubtless consider it to be quite natural that, for example, prayer is answered just in the measure and degree of its 'faith'. Much also that now goes under the label of 'spiritual healing' would fall into its natural place as a power of the mind.

Apart from physical science there has sprung up within the present century a science of Mind, Psychology, which has already disclosed to us hitherto unsuspected depths and actions of the human mind. There are doubtless many discoveries to be made in this direction which will tend still further to remove elements of superstition and supernaturalism which still cling to the obscure actions of the mind upon matter. The existence and action of the subconscious is, in this direction, as great a discovery and a revolution of ideas as is the discovery of the inner constitution of the atom of physical matter. Professor Eddington in his work just referred to says:

"Consciousness is not sharply defined, but fades into subconsciousness; and beyond that we must postulate something indefinite but yet continuous with our mental nature. This I take to be the world-stuff. We liken it to our conscious feelings because, now that we are convinced of the formal and symbolic character of the entities of physics, there is nothing else to liken it to. . . . It is difficult for the matter-of-fact physicist to accept the view that the substratum of everything is of mental character. But no one can deny that mind is the first and most direct thing in our experience, and all else is remote inference " (pp. 280, 281).

This is indeed a jump from physics to the metaphysics so much despised last century by the matter-of-fact physicist, who did not know that even then he was an unconscious metaphysician. But now it would appear that the new physics leads directly to metaphysical conclusions which are as old as any philosophy of which we have any records. Thus in the *Brihad-âranyaka Upanishad* (1, 5, 3) we read :

" It is with the mind, truly, that one sees. It is with the mind that one hears. Desire, imagination, doubt, faith, lack of faith, steadfastness, lack of steadfastness, shame, meditation, fear—all this is truly mind. Therefore even if one is touched on his back, he discerns it with the mind."

The direct action of mind on mind, as in hypnotism and telepathy, is also giving us a deeper insight into the super-physical—previously designated the supernatural.

We might, as a preliminary classification, grade the " stuff— " though substance, *i.e.*, that which sub-stands, would appear to be a better word—as follows: physical matter, ether, mind-stuff, Spirit.

We may conceive of these as being at root all one Substance, but we must not conceive of that Substance as being in any way analogous to physical matter as being *substantial*. What it may be in its own nature as ' Spirit ' is utterly incomprehensible. Philosophically it is the Absolute ; theologically it is God—or perhaps this would be repudiated by the theologian as being pantheism. Yet if God is " all and in all ", what else can it be ?

> " In this high consideration it is found that all is through and from God himself, and that it is his own substance, which is himself, and he hath created it out of himself ; and that the evil belongeth to the forming and mobility ; and the good to the love " (Jacob Böhme, *The Three Principles*, Preface).

In any case we recognise that the difference between physical matter as such, and the Ether which is the more immediate substance of which it is composed, is so great that any attempt to define what Mind is as one further or deeper remove from the Ether, is seen to be quite beyond our powers. Yet we are compelled to conceive of Cosmic Mind as being at least as 'substantial' as the Ether. We are compelled to conceive of it as a *force*, for it produces, at least in our own bodies—and most probably through the intermediary of the Ether—action on physical matter. Moreover we are compelled to conceive of telepathy as being in some sense analogous to wireless waves. Some *medium* transmits the thought vibration, which, as a vibration, or any other *form* of motion in the root substance, must certainly, be as definite a 'thing' on its own plane as are the wireless waves in the Ether.

Even thus will the super-natural, and the superstitions attached to it, be pushed further and further back. And if the theologian tells us that God is "in substance and essence" above and beyond our deepest conceptions of any ultimate Substance of the manifested or phenomenal world, we shall reply that at least in all His operations in that world He must act only by and through natural law; and that in fact what we call natural law must in this regard be the law of His own Nature and Substance from which He will be indistinguishable. If He must be regarded as a personal Being, acting very much as we ourselves act, only with infinitely more knowledge and power: we are at least told that "in Him there is no variableness neither shadow of turning", and that is precisely what we recognise in the operation of natural law.

Thus we see HIS—or ITS—very Substance and Being as the Substance of the outer world of phenomena; and we partake of it in our own bodies, whether physical, etherical, mental, or spiritual. Moreover, to the extent that we de-individualise our consciousness and allow it to expand into Cosmic Consciousness, so do we reach in still fuller and fuller degree that ONE which is the Root of the subjective eternal Self as well as the objective temporal personality.

Thus we are told in the old Hermetic Script:

> "If, then, thou dost not make thyself like unto God, thou canst not know Him. For like is knowable to like alone. Make, then, thyself to grow to the same stature as the Greatness which transcends all measure; leap forth from every body; transcend all Time; become Eternity; and thus shalt thou know God."

And who among our theologians who discourse so learnedly of God as being this, that, and the other, can claim to have done this? Paraphrasing the saying of the old Chinese philosopher, Lâo Tsze, and also the *Upanishads*, verily we may say: "He who knows God tells it not; he who tells it knows Him not."

Let us now take a brief survey of the past in order the better to understand the present and to forecast the future.

A Survey of the Past

We pass back over the pages of history and we see the first beginnings, the growth, maturity, and final decay of innumerable systems of religious beliefs and ritual practices, from the crude animistic fetish of the primitive savage to the elaborate and ornate ritual of the Romish Church to-day: borrowed —without acknowledgment—from the earlier symbolism and practices of the 'Pagan' mythology of Egypt, Greece, Rome, and even of India. One might almost say that whatever is connected historically with Christian theology and ritual is entirely derived from pagan sources, and has no connection whatsoever with the teachings of Jesus of Nazareth.[1]

In vast waste places of the Globe—once the scene of activity of mighty nations, but now overgrown by the primeval forest, or buried under the sandy billows of the desert, or still standing in magnificent ruins—we see the remains of altars and shrines and stately temples dedicated, in the not very remote

[1] For a fuller statement and summary of our present knowledge in this connection readers may be referred to the work of Arthur Weigall, *The Paganism in our Christianity*.

past—as we now understand the age of mankind—to the worship of this, that, or the other God; Sun Gods, Moon Gods, Serpent Gods, Fire Gods, Gods and Goddesses; Gods who must be worshipped and propitiated; Gods satisfied with nothing less than a sacrificial victim—animal or human, but always with the shedding of blood—culminating sometimes in the idea of the God himself being slain and resurrected—as for example Mithras, Krishna, Osiris, Horus, and many others before the time of the deified Christian Saviour.

Gods, Gods, ever more, Gods innumerable; their names would fill a volume; names which for the most part mean nothing to anyone now-a-days, but which once represented the beliefs of untold millions, and the dominance of priesthoods holding unlimited power and wealth through the fostered superstitions of ignorant multitudes.

Is it any different to-day? No—and Yes.

Let not anyone think that our present temples and fanes, or the beliefs which they represent, are any more permanent than these ancient ruins. A million years hence—and what is a million years in the whole history of Man?—where will all these be?

Yet even so, in the eyes of the seer and the mystic that seemingly distant period is *here and now*; it is already discounted in his estimate of *Reality*. It has not yet taken form and objectivity in the normal consciousness of Humanity; it has not yet come into view in the series of moving pictures which pass across the screen of time and space: the *event* being no more than the momentary picture flashed on the screen, only to disappear as instantaneously as it has appeared.

"The Moving Finger writes; and, having writ,
Moves on: nor all your Piety nor Wit
Shall lure it back to cancel half a Line,
Nor all your tears wash out a Word of it."

And even so, apprehending this deeper truth, we give heed to present forms and formulas only in so far as they can serve their time and generation in the minds of those whose vision extends no farther; those to whom it is not yet given "to know the mysteries of the kingdom of heaven"—mysteries which are quite outside the relations of time and space, or the forms and doctrines of any religion whatsoever.

Through all this welter of Gods in the past,

and the modern conflict and strife of creeds and dogmas, there is one thing that stands out very clearly. Each and every *formulated* conception of the unseen Power or Powers of the Universe, whether monotheistic or polytheistic, has hitherto been purely anthropomorphic. Always and ever man has created his God or Gods in his own likeness, and has ascribed to them like consciousness, like passions, like motives to those which he himself possesses.

It is true that higher and more philosophical concepts have never been absent in the teachings of saints and sages and philosophers and mystics in all ages ; but these have never found their way into *institutional* religion, or have only done so in a grossly perverted form.

I will deal with these higher concepts presently ; in the meanwhile let us consider the traditional Christian theology, since it is that with which we are the most concerned in this Western part of the Globe.

The God of Christendom

Nothing is clearer in connection with Christian theology than that it was formulated by those whose outlook on the universe, or Nature, was vastly different from ours of to-day. It was in fact made by those whose knowledge and concepts were of the most rudimentary character; when this world was considered by them to be the one and only place with which 'God' was concerned; when the Earth was commonly believed to be flat; when the Sun and the Moon and the Stars were all supposed to rotate round it, and to have been created for the special benefit of Man; when no idea existed as to the distances or sizes of these heavenly bodies: the stars being merely so many points of light, more or less bright.

It is commonly supposed that up to the time of Copernicus (1473–1543) nothing had been known about the rotundity of the Earth or its revolution round the Sun. But Aristarchus, 260 B.C., had taught this, and the rotundity of the Earth was well known to many Greek writers. The fact was that the makers of the Christian dogmas put the Scripture narrative before everything else. Thus St. Augustine naïvely remarks that: "It is impossible that there should be inhabitants on the opposite side of the Earth, since no such race is recorded by Scripture among the descendents of Adam."

The theology was formulated when the Old Testament was accepted as the personally inspired word of the Jewish God Jehovah, and the account of the creation in Genesis was held to be literally true—hence the doctrine of the Fall of Man, of original sin, and of the necessity—carried over from pagan sources—of a propitiatory offering. The "only begotten Son of God" had to atone for the sins of the world by incarnating and shedding his blood on the Cross, as so many previous 'Saviours' are reputed to have done.

In the person of Jesus of Nazareth these allegories were literalised by the Christian theology makers, and finally, at the various Ecumenical Councils, were hardened into their traditional form as they have been handed down to us.

If we take the Gospels and the Acts of the Apostles to be mainly historical—which is very doubtful—we see that the immediate followers of Jesus utterly misunderstood and materialised his teachings and his mission. They looked for an immediate Second Coming, for the "last day" when the Earth and the Sea would yield up the physical bodies of all humanity from the time of Adam; when the personal Devil would be finally overcome and cast into Hell with all the 'heathen' and the unbelievers, whilst the 'saints' would share in the glories of the new Heaven and the new Earth.

Strange to say this naïve belief survives even to-day; nor has there been any century of the Christian era in which the Second Coming has not been expected, and even prophesied for a certain date, which numberless credulous 'believers' have confidently accepted.

As regards the teaching of Jesus, which was essentially that of the Fatherhood of God and the Brotherhood of Man, the Christian nations have always treated the 'heathen', the coloured races in particular, as if they were of no account in the sight of God—witness, for example, the conflict over the emancipation of the slaves. The original incentive to missionary effort—whatever it may be now—was based on the idea that the benighted heathen had to be 'saved' in the orthodox

Christian manner, otherwise he was irretrievably doomed to Hell. Indeed it was not the heathen only, but even a Church member could not be certain that his fellow member was "one of the elect". Of course he could be quite sure about himself generally. But this same doctrine of election, even now held by some, has sent thousands into our lunatic asylums.

The Roman Catholic Church still claims to hold the keys of Heaven, and regards the members of all other Christian Churches as being excluded therefrom.

Now it is not to the point that hundreds of thousands still accept this original crude theology. It is not to the 'tail' that we must look for the religion of the future. The old orthodoxy is very much in the melting-pot to-day. It is hardly a question even as to whether it will survive another century. The question is as to what will take its place. What concept of Deity, what concepts of the Universe or Nature will result from our enlarged modern knowledge? What concepts of *himself* will the enlightened member of the Race formulate out of the extraordinary advancement of knowledge which is now resulting from scientific discoveries and modern scholarship?

The established hierarchy of traditional theology has always fought and will doubtless continue to fight against the rising tide of knowledge. History shows us that even the most primitive ideas when supported by a powerful and wealthy priesthood are exceedingly difficult to uproot; and nothing in the average mind dies harder than religious superstition and traditional belief. The Church of Rome will have nothing to do with 'Modernism', and its adherents are forbidden free investigation in certain directions, or to read books which have been placed on the *Index*.

Three hundred years ago it was astronomy which threatened to overthrow the teachings of the Church, and Bruno was burnt at the stake for teaching what is now common knowledge. Galileo only escaped the same fate by recanting what he knew to be true. One hundred years ago it was geology which challenged the Scripture record and the cherished belief in the Genesis narrative. The Devil was said to have put the fossils there to deceive mankind. There are still a few good people who profess to believe that. Since the time of Darwin and Huxley it has been biology to which the conflict has been transferred, and *evolution* is now the word which is anathema. And so the story goes on.

We can have no quarrel with the sincere believer who finds his spiritual sustenance in the old doctrine of Man's Fall and Redemption, and consoles himself with the thought that one brief life well spent—or even badly spent if he can obtain priestly absolution before he dies—will ensure for him an endless life in Paradise. Yet this is a soul-killing doctrine.

We have nothing to say either against those who find inspiration in an elaborate ritual—vestments, and masses, music and incense, *et hoc genus omne*—and may even think that these are the principal elements of religion, and that God himself takes a delight in them. But why associate these with the simple teachings of Jesus of Nazareth? Who can imagine Jesus, or Paul, or Peter in a cope, or a mitre, or a chasuble? "The hour cometh when neither in this mountain, nor in Jerusalem shall ye worship the Father. Ye worship that which ye know not." The very idea that God requires to be worshipped and propitiated is a survival of primitive anthropomorphism.

All these institutional practices may be 'Christianity' as it has come to be known historically; but they certainly do not belong to the religion of Jesus Christ, nor even to that of Paul—the great Apostle to the 'Gentiles'—whose fundamental teaching was "Christ *in* you". Paul might have been expected to quote Jesus continually as his authority, but, strange to say, he never quotes him, with the single exception of *Acts* xx, 35: "It is more blessed to give than to receive"—a saying which is not found in the Gospels.

It is food for thought also that Philo, who was contemporary with Jesus, never mentions him, though he uses the term 'Logos', and also "only begotten Son". Both these terms are pre-Christian, as is also the doctrine of the Trinity. They are pre-Christian philosophical concepts, and were not 'divinely revealed' by the coming of Christ. They were appropriated by the Church, like so many other things, from pagan sources.

And so we may leave the orthodox theology with those to whose mental limitations it is best suited, and proceed to note the groundwork for our conception of Man and the Universe which our modern science and our modern scholarship and philosophy provides, and which must inevitably influence and determine the religion of the future.

Astronomy

Let us commence with astronomy, since it was the first real science to threaten the traditional theology by enlarging man's knowledge of the extent and nature of the universe in which he finds himself.

Can we with our modern knowledge conceive in the remotest degree what a monstrous thing it was in the year 1600, when Bruno was burnt at the stake, for anyone to assert that the Earth was round, not flat, and that the Sun and all the heavenly bodies did not revolve round the Earth for its own special benefit but the Earth round the Sun ? Such assertions were not merely contrary to common sense, to what everyone could see for themselves, but worse still, they were contrary to Holy Scripture. They appeared to cut away the very foundations of Christian belief. When the Inquisitors were invited by Galileo to look through his telescope and see for themselves the Satellites of Jupiter revolving round that Planet, they refused to do so. The thing was impossible, for it was not in Holy Scripture ; and moreover, we had no right to pry into what was not there revealed to us.

What does our astronomical knowledge disclose to us to-day ? What are our present conceptions of the nature and extent of the visible universe ?

The number of stars which could be seen with the great 100-inch reflecting telescope at Mount Wilson in California, is estimated to be about fifteen-hundred million—a few million more or less don't matter. But that is by no means the end of the story. The new relativity theory gives us a universe which is "finite but unbounded".[1] Space—as disclosed by the material world—(the reservation is important) is supposed to be curved, so that if one were able to set out on a journey into space, apparently in a straight course, and were to travel with the speed of light, namely, 186,000 miles per second, or nearly 6,000,000,000,000 miles per annum, one would find oneself possibly at the end of something like 100,000,000,000 years—according to

[1] This phrase "finite but unbounded" represents what is supposed to be an absolutely new conception resulting from the four-dimensional mathematics of the Relativity Theory. In *Isis Unveiled*, however, the work of that marvellously informed woman, Mme. H. P. Blavatsky, and published in 1877, we find the following sentence. "But notwithstanding that the world of matter is boundless for us, it still is finite" (Vol. I, p. 7).

present calculations—back on the same spot from which we started. As the schoolboy said when he was asked to define a circle: it is a line which meets its other end without ending.

The nearest star to our Earth, *a* Centauri, is 4⅓ light years distant. Sirius, the brightest star in the heavens, 26 times as bright as the Sun, is 8.7 light years away. The Pleiades some 325 light years. But these are comparatively near neighbours. The great star cluster in the constellation of Hercules, which contains fully 35,000 stars as bright as our Sun, and some more than a thousand times brighter, is about 36,000 light years away. The whole of our system of stars, known as the Galactic system, approximates to the form of a flattened disc, with a thickness about one-eighth of the diameter; our Sun being a very considerable distance from the centre. The diameter of this disc is estimated to be somewhere in the order of 300,000 light years, and the thickness about 37,500 light years.

But in addition to our Galactic system it is estimated that there are something like two million extra-galactic nebulae visible with the 100-inch telescope. Each of these is either a system of stars—a universe in itself—

or one in the making. Some of these nebulae have been estimated to be as much as 140 million light years away. Taking the Einstein theory as a basis, it is estimated that the whole universe is about one-thousand-million times as big as the part of space visible with the 100-inch telescope.

In this vast universe, our own Solar System—taking the orbit of Neptune as its limit—is but an insignificant atom. Sir J. H. Jeans, in his little work "*Eos, or the Wider Aspects of Cosmogony*", estimates that if the whole number of stars in the universe were represented by grains of sand spread over England, they would make a layer many hundreds of yards in depth; and that our Earth would be only one-millionth part of one such grain.

What concern, then, are our little worldly affairs to any supposed Cosmic Deity, whether inside or outside of this vast universe; whether it was all created by the word of His mouth in six days, or in six hundred thousand million years? What concern can even the existence of our little speck of matter be to such an inconceivable Being—let alone the idea that we may pray to Him for rain or for fine weather, and ask Him to bless our crops and our battle-ships? These figures utterly transcend the power of our minds to grasp; how then can we possibly conceive of a Being who made all this by a simple *fiat*, and who is supposed to be omnipresent and omniscient in this vast universe, let alone the idea that He requires to be *worshipped* by the microbes on this little microscopic object which we call our Earth. Conceivably millions of such little specks of matter as our Globe could come into and go out of existence in the equally ungraspable extension of '*Time*' without even touching the consciousness of such a Being; just as millions of microscopic lives come into and go out of existence in our own bodies every minute without our being in the least aware of them.

No: the moment we begin to think in any sense cosmically instead of parochially, the postulating of a personal God who is this, that, and the other—not to speak of His opponent the personal Devil—appears as the mere childish beginnings of Man's effort to understand his existence and his place in the Cosmos, and his own larger spiritual nature.

But let it not be thought that this is either pessimism or atheism. There is another aspect of this question. How is it that *we*, mere microbes crawling on the surface of this million-millionth speck of matter, can thus discern, and measure, and weigh and analyse the incalculable millions of Suns and Universes scattered through space ? Must there not be something infinitely great in Man, greater than any of these physical dimensions, that he is able to do this—something that is only *shadowed* in these achievements ?

"I am somehow receptive of the great soul, and thereby I do overlook the sun and the stars, and feel them to be but the fair accidents and effects which change and pass" (Emerson, *The Oversoul*).

Must not *Mind*, which can thus compass the universe of matter, be infinitely greater than that which it thus compasses ? Must we not postulate also a *Cosmic Mind* which brings all this forth in its own imaging or imagination ? This Cosmic Mind was conceived of in Greek philosophy as the *Logos*, about which we shall say more presently.

Nothing is more certain than that the individual can only exercise a faculty which is derived from something *cosmic* in the first instance. Like the atom of physical matter which is simply a limited and individual aspect of a potency residing in the cosmic Ether: the mind of the individual man can only be a limited and partial aspect of the potency of Cosmic Mind. All our modern psychology and philosophy tends to show that even the individual mind is to a large extent in its own sphere, the *creator* of the objective world, and of time and space. "Intellectuality and materiality," Bergson tells us, "have been constituted by reciprocal adaptation. Both are derived from a wider and higher form of existence." [1]

But we must enquire presently whether even intellect is Man's highest faculty; whether, indeed, it is in any way fitted to grasp *Reality*. Are the physical dimensions and measurements which the mind cannot overpass in any *formulated* concept, of any real value as criteria of Man's nature and status in the Universe? Does not their very excess destroy their value?

Let us turn for a moment from these *outward* dimensions of space and look *inwards*. If the macrocosm discloses these immensities, what of the microcosm?

[1] *Creative Evolution*, p. 127.

The Constitution of Matter

About the year 1704 Sir Isaac Newton wrote:

"It seems probable to me that God in the beginning formed matter in solid, massy, hard, impenetrable, movable particles, of such sizes and figures, and with such other properties, and in such proportion to space as most to conduce to the end for which He formed them; and that these primitive particles, being solids, are incomparably harder than any porous body compounded of them; even so very hard as never to wear or break to pieces; no ordinary power being able to divide what God Himself made one in the first creation."

Great as was Sir Isaac Newton's intellect, we now know that this conception of the atom of matter was wrong in every respect. The atom is not a solid body; it is mainly composed of space, just as the Solar System as a whole may be said to be. It is neither hard nor impenetrable, and it does wear and break to pieces. As for the theological idea which he introduces, we need hardly say that no physicist nowadays would consider that to be relevant to his conceptions as to the nature of matter.

The atom or molecule of physical matter was known last century—before the possibility of its break-up or the nature of its constituents was even guessed at—to be exceedingly minute. It was estimated that it would take something like 250,000,000 placed close together to cover the length of one inch. One pint of water contains a far greater number of atoms than there are pints in all the oceans of the world. One cubic centimeter of air—less than the top of one's little finger—is estimated to contain about 28 million million million molecules. An ordinary electric light vacuum bulb encloses a space of about 150 cubic centimetres; and if a minute hole were made in it so that one million molecules could enter per second, a simple calculation will show that it would take rather more than 133 million years to fill the bulb.

But it is now known that the atom is composed of a number of electrical particles called electrons and protons, and that these are inconceivably smaller than the atom itself: so much so that they are comparable, as regards their relative size and the distances between them, to the sizes and distances of the Sun and Planets of the Solar System. The atom is in fact conceived to be a Solar System in miniature, with the proton, or positive electrical particle as a central nucleus round which the electrons, or negative particles, revolve in orbits. This present theory, however, fascinating and simple as it appears to be, is even now in question. We may, however, work on it in the meanwhile as not merely being explanatory of certain facts, but also as giving us some sort of a mental picture corresponding to those facts.

The present data show the electron to be something like 100,000 times smaller than the atom; so that in comparison with the whole space occupied by the atom it is only about $\frac{1}{500 \text{ billionth}}$ of that space. The electrons have been compared to a few gnats flying about in a space as great as a cathedral. If the electron were magnified to the size of a halfpenny, its relative distance from the proton round which we suppose it to revolve, and which is about the same size, would be one mile.

Conceive of one halfpenny revolving round another one mile distant, and you have a picture of the hydrogen atom. We may compare this with the Solar System in the following manner. If we had to make a model of the System to a scale in which the size of the Earth was represented by a halfpenny, the Sun would be 326 yards away, whilst Neptune, the outermost planet, would be rather more than five and a half miles distant. As regards the atom, however, we must bear in mind that the electrons are revolving in their orbits with enormous velocities, so that the halfpenny electron might go round its central nucleus something like twenty or thirty thousand times in one second. It is thus practically an impenetrable ring, just as when we revolve a ball at the end of a string very rapidly in a circle, we see it as a ring. Matter is only *solid* because of its intense atomic motion.

Such are the refinements of our modern scientific instruments and processes that we can now photograph the tracks of atoms and electrons.

The various chemical atoms have different numbers of electrons which determine the characteristics of their chemical properties. Thus the hydrogen atom has only one electron; the oxygen has eight; and at the other end of the scale the uranium atom has ninety-two. Thus we see that "matter is mainly composed of space." How very different in the light of this knowledge do we find the *reality* of the material world to be from its *appearance.*

These figures, like the complementary astronomical figures, altogether dwarf our imagination. But even so, we have by no means got to the end of the matter—literally *matter.* The electrons themselves are doubtless compound bodies. Sir J. J. Thomson has put forward the view that:

> "If we compare the atom with its electrons to a solar system, we may compare an electron or a positive particle to the centre of a nebula, and regard the electron as surrounded by an atmosphere of small particles. . . . These considerations suggest that just as matter is made up of molecules, and molecules are made up of electrons and positive particles, this is not the end of the story, there are still other worlds to conquer, the worlds which build up the electrons and positive particles."

Where, then, can there be an end in this *inner* direction of space? Any 'space', however minute, is conceivably divisible, and re-divisible, *ad infinitum.*

What a mighty thing, therefore, is our present physical body when measured by the standard of these microcosmic dimensions. Shall we not set them off against the macrocosmic dimensions of astronomy, and say that the one cancels out the other, and that perhaps *at root* extension in space has no ' reality ' at all; that our consciousness makes it, and can transcend it?

Professor Eddington tells us that:—

> " If we eliminated all the unfilled space in a man's body and collected his protons and electrons into one mass, the man would be reduced to a speck just visible with a magnifying glass." [1]

According to these present conceptions the whole universe might very well be the physical body of some great Cosmic Being, and all the suns and worlds mere atoms in that body. But that is no new idea. Swedenborg taught that the universe was in the form of a man: though perhaps he did not quite mean it in that sense. But the conception of the Archetypal Man as containing the whole universe within himself is one of the oldest concepts of the more occult philosophy. We

[1] *The Nature of the Physical World*, p. 1.

find it clearly stated by Jacob Böhme, that unrivalled spiritual seer. Thus he says:

> "And we declare unto you that the eternal Being, and also this world, is *like* man: The *eternity* generateth nothing but that which is like itself; for there is nothing in it but is like it, and it is unchangeable, or else it would *pass away*, or it would come to be *some other* thing, and that cannot be. And as you find man to be, just so is the eternity. *All is in man*, both heaven and earth, stars, and elements" (*The Threefold Life of Man*, VI, 46, 47).

As for "the space within the atom," we read in the *Yoga Vâsishtha* of Indian literature that:

> "There are vast worlds all placed away within the hollows of each atom, multifarious as the motes in sunbeams."

Modern astronomy may be said to have become atomic, and modern conceptions of the atom astronomical.

The Age of the Earth

We may now turn from the consideration of spatial quantities to that of time. How old is the Solar System, and more particularly our little speck of matter?

We have two means of estimating the age of the Earth: the data derived from astronomy and that derived from geology.

The discovery by modern science of the constitution of physical matter, of the break up of the atom and the consequent liberation of enormous stores of energy in the form of radiation, has placed a powerful method of calculation in the hands of both the astronomer and the geologist. Whereas it was previously thought that the energy radiated from the Sun must in some way be accounted for by combustion, and calculations on that basis could only give it a life of some ten or fifteen million years, the knowledge of the energy stored up in the atom now enables us to reckon by millions of millions of years.

Radiation means loss of mass: annihilation of the atom. The atomic annihilation of one pound of coal per week would give us as much energy as is now available from the combustion of the five millions of tons of coal which are mined every week in the British Isles. A single drop of oil would take the largest liner across the Atlantic.

We know the mass of the Sun, and we can also calculate the amount of energy which is radiated from its surface. It is therefore easy to calculate the equivalent loss of mass. This loss is at the rate of 250 million tons per minute; yet at this enormous rate the Sun would last for another fifteen million million years, while its present age is probably between five and eight million million years.

It is perhaps easier to calculate the approximate age of the Sun or even of distant stars, from the given data, than to calculate the age of the Earth. It is generally conceded that the Earth and the other Planets have been, in some unknown manner, thrown off from the Sun. The theory which appears to be most in favour to-day with astronomers being that the near approach of a passing star caused a large arm or streamer of matter to be drawn out of the Sun by gravitational action: the Sun being at that time a gaseous nebula. This protuberance subsequently condensed and detached itself as a planet. A similar action is supposed to happen to the Planets, whereby their satellites are formed. All this, however, is pure speculation, and by no means satisfactory even at that. Occult science has quite a different teaching, which however would be out of place here. Moreover there is nothing to show us how many million million years ago it was since this may have happened. We must turn to geology for more direct evidence of the age of the Earth.

The data from which geologists can draw their conclusions are very varied. Calculations have been made from the accumulation of salt in the oceans; from the thickness of the sedimentary and other formations, but more recently, and perhaps more reliably, from an analysis of the radio-active contents of some of the rocks of the earth's crust.

The uranium and thorium ores, which are radio-active, go through a series of slow transformations, the end products of which are helium and lead. The rate of transformation is fairly well known, so that these radio-active materials act as a kind of time-keeper for the earth. The conclusions arrived at by this method point to a period which is somewhere between 1,600 million years as a minimum and 3,000 million years as a maximum. Other geological evidence is more or less in accord with these figures; but once we have passed, say 1,000 million years in our estimate, a few millions, or even a few hundred millions, matters very little. In any case we must reckon by hundreds of millions, and Bishop Usher's 6,000 years is—no-when.

To suppose that Man came into existence on this Earth full-grown, and at the word of a personal Creator, is another of those primitive ideas which can find no support or corroboration in our actual knowledge of the processes of Nature and of biological evolution, though it still survives in the minds of millions who profess the 'Christian faith', and it is the authoritative teaching of both the Roman and Anglican Churches.

But with biology, as it has already been with astronomy and geology, it can only be a question of time for the known facts to be universally recognised by everyone but the extremely ignorant—or the extremely bigoted. As regards the *Genesis* narrative there will then be two alternatives: its total rejection, or its allegorical interpretation. The theology which still clings to that narrative in its literal acceptation is in fact already a lost cause.

A very mild attempt to recognise the allegorical nature of the narrative is already in evidence with apologists in certain quarters. It is said that the 'days' of creation do not mean actual days of the week, but periods of time which may possibly extend over thousands or even millions of years. So far so good; but there is a great deal more to be said in the matter.

I will attempt a brief outline of this immediately; but first of all let us look at the biological facts.

There was undoubtedly a time in the early formation of this Globe when no organic forms whatsoever could possibly have existed. Whatever theory we may accept as to the probable or possible origin of the Globe as a throw-off from the Sun or otherwise, we may say that literally it was, "in the beginning", and for millions of years, "waste and void", and that "there went up a great mist from the earth, and watered the whole face of the ground".

Now there appears to be very little doubt that the first organic forms of life, the primitive protoplasm and the unicellular protozoa, arose in the slime of the warm tropical oceans. From these primitive cells the whole of our flora and fauna have evolved during the course of incalculable ages. No one at all acquainted with the facts of the case is inclined to dispute this to-day. We have not merely the indelible records of the geological strata and the fossils to show us the gradual evolution of more and more complex organisms in ever increasing variety, but each individual human being to-day commences his existence as a primitive cell, and recapitulates during his nine months gestation the whole biological evolutionary process.

The various stages of that evolution may be represented broadly in the following diagram. They are the stages for the Race as well as for the individual embryo.

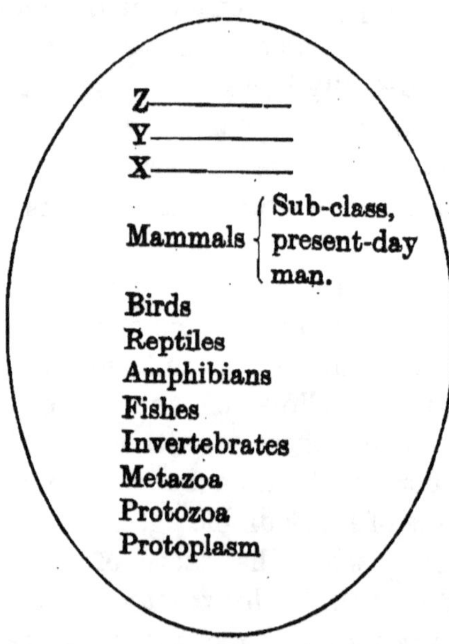

We may put X, Y, Z as three stages of as yet unknown development: for the process still goes on. Also we may enclose the whole in an egg to signify that Man—in so far as he is *physical*, and limited in his consciousness to the physical world—is as yet only in the gestation stage as regards his future development as a *cosmic* being, with cosmic consciousness. He has still to come out of the shell of matter with which he has encased himself during his 'fall'. He is still a crustacean clinging to a rock, and not a free-swimming creature in the larger world of the cosmic Ether.

Man having thus evolved his physical body through all the lower organic kingdoms—and perchance even through the mineral [1]—and being now the highest representative of the organic process, we may consider that he was as much in view from the beginning as a full-grown product as is the oak from the acorn, or the full-grown individual man from the germ-cell.

But was, or is, the ultimate end merely the

[1] "I died from the mineral and became a plant;
I died from the plant and re-appeared as an animal;
I died from the animal and became a man;
Wherefore then should I fear? When did I grow less by dying?"
—JALALU'D-DIN RUMI.

evolution of a physical body for Man? Assuredly not—at all events from the point of view of religion. We are necessarily taking that point of view in this work, and religion necessarily implies not merely that man survives his physical body but also that he has a *spiritual* nature. What this implies I will deal with more in detail immediately; but meanwhile we may note that *we do not know* why in the one case an oak should result, and in the other case a human being. Nevertheless we are compelled to postulate an inner active principle moulding the 'dead' chemical matter into these innumerable other forms which we recognise as being 'living'. That inner principle in fact we term *Life*.

So far as the biological process on this Earth is concerned, as soon as the matter of the Globe has reached a certain state or stage of chemical organisation, *Life* begins to manifest itself in organisms scarcely distinguishable from complex chemical molecules, but yet distinct in this one respect, that they have the power of *self-initiated movement*. We distinguish them as living organisms—or sometimes simply as living matter—because they are the most primitive or simplest form of organised matter—more complex than the chemical atom or molecule—in which we can recognise this self-initiated movement. What we commonly call 'dead' matter is, in its aggregated forms, only moved by external impacts. What we call 'living' matter moves itself by internal impulse.

That is the bare definition of Life so far as its connection with physical matter is concerned. But Life as we know it in ourselves is something which exhibits infinitely more than the power to move or mould matter. It includes consciousness, mind, will, emotion; and, as we have seen from the quotation I have already given from Huxley (p. 14) there is no conceivable connection between these and the mere mechanical properties of so-called dead matter. Thus the first expression of Life recognisable by us is movement. We might perhaps say that the highest expression is Love.

The term 'origin of life' which is so commonly used in scientific works is quite misleading. What should be spoken of is *the origin of organic forms of life.* Organic forms *manifest* the informing life, but they do not originate it. How can they? If we postulate that it is matter itself which moves itself, then matter itself *is* life, and we can never speak of *dead* matter. These terms of course came into use when matter was considered to be nothing more than Newton's "solid, massy, hard, impenetrable, movable particles." Our present knowledge that matter is derived from and composed of a more universal *Substance*—which may even be "mind-stuff" itself, not to speak of Spirit—puts a totally different complexion on the question. The ultimate Cosmic Substance may be *living substance*—may be Life itself.

If I make a vortex-ring in water, the ring is distinguishable *qua* ring, that is to say as a *form*, from the substance of the water. It is true that I cannot distinguish the form by physical sight unless I introduce a little colouring matter into the water. How then does it come about that 'I' can distinguish physical matter from the Ether of which the electrons and protons are composed: very possibly being something analogous to vortex-rings therein? My physical body is built up of these, which, from the analogy of the vortex-rings in water, should be indistinguishable from the substance of which they are composed. I, then, as being the living cognising subject, am either distinct from both physical matter and the substance out of which it is formed, or else that substance is at root *myself*.

Matter in its atomic constitution is an organised form of the substance of the Ether just as much as are the more complex 'organic' forms which are organised out of the simpler atoms and molecules. They are all one *Substance*: how then shall we say that some of the forms are organised by Life whilst others are not? If we postulate that Life is something quite distinct from Substance then we must say that Life as it were *comes in* only so soon as a certain complexity of physical matter has been reached. But the real fact is that it is only when a certain degree of organisation of matter has been reached that we are able to recognise the self-initiated action of Life. If we conceive of the Ether as being a dead substance, how could it possibly organise, or be organised into form, unless Life acted *upon* it? The alternative is that Life is intrinsic in the nature of the Ether, or in something much deeper or more cosmic than the Ether.

The new physics has already entirely de-materialised our concepts of matter; and we see clearly that we have two things to deal with: a Root Substance—which science at present calls the Ether of space—and an active *Principle* which we call Life. We are here in fact face to face with the choice between the duality of Life and Substance, or the monistic view that they are at root, and in a last analysis, one and the same. In any case it is not physical matter *as such* which contains the potentiality of evolving into the forms of living organisms.

Are we then compelled to make a choice between Monism or Dualism ? I think not; but at the same time how are we possibly to distinguish in any final analysis between Life and living Substance ? It is simpler to speak of the Life as if it were an attribute of the Substance; or conversely of Substance as an attribute of Life. Indeed, if we call the Life 'God', we are compelled to postulate that God and Substance are not two things, otherwise God is not "all and in all." The same applies if we simply call it the Absolute. The universe in its totality, visible and invisible, is *one Substance and one Life*, infinite, uncreated and eternal, whatever name we may give to it in its unitary nature.

Returning for a moment to the origin of physical forms of life on this Globe, we cannot say at what exact period—how many hundreds of millions of years ago—life began to mould the first organic forms ; nor can we say at what point in the process Man came to be distinguished from the mere animal—whether ape or otherwise—as *homo sapiens.* There was no such precise point. Man is distinguished from the animal by his superior mentality, and to a certain extent by his nascent spirituality. But the incoming of Mind—the manifestation through the organism of that particular attribute of the Cosmic Life, already existing in that Life in a supreme degree—has been a gradual process, and is in fact as yet by no means complete ; whilst the real spiritual nature of Man—also already existing in a supreme degree in the One Life—is hardly as yet in evidence at all in humanity as a whole.

We have records of primitive man which appear to go back several millions of years ; but there is no authentic certainty in the matter, for we do not know the age of the geological strata in which these are found ; as for example those of the Neanderthal man.

In what respects is the highest type of man to-day distinguished from primitive man of the flint or stone age ? In what respects does he manifest more fully the attributes of the One Cosmic Life ?

Undoubtedly in the first instance he manifests an amazing increase in the powers of mind or intellect; the power to formulate *ideas*, both abstract and concrete, the power to analyse and the power to synthesise not merely the phenomena of the objective world of Nature, but also the subjective world of his own mind and emotions. He formulates science and philosophy, and an enquiry into the limitations of his own knowledge. He is infinitely more self-conscious.

But that is by no means all. He has discovered that he has feelings and emotions which are something much more than, and essentially different from, mental concepts. The emotions of love and hatred are not intellectual; neither is his sense of esthetic values. The whole *colouring* which he gives to his mental concepts as well as to his external percepts, belongs to a region of his nature which transcends mind. In short he has discovered that he has a *soul*; or, as it is sometimes termed, a spiritual nature.

But it is not he who evolves that nature; it is that nature which evolves him—in so far as he is represented by a succession of individual forms.

It is just here that we must break away from conventional ideas of Man; and more particularly from conventional religious ideas and dogmas. The new physics and the new biology, of which I have given such a brief sketch, are here, if rightly understood and applied, of immense service to—shall we say—the new religion. Just as the concepts of the new physics de-materialise matter, so also must we de-materialise Man; and just as they de-individualise the physical atom, and refer it back to a Cosmic Substance, so also must we de-individualise our concepts of Man, of ourselves, and refer the individual back to a Cosmic Life.

Let us now turn our attention to this larger aspect of Man's origin and nature.

Spiritual Man

What is Spirit?

Spirit is only another name for the one Infinite, Eternal, Uncreated Root and Source of all that ever was, is, or can be. It is the ONE LIFE and the ONE SUBSTANCE.

> "Never the Spirit was born; the Spirit shall cease to be never;
> Never was time it was not; End and Beginning are dreams!
> Birthless and deathless and changeless remaineth the Spirit for ever;
> Death hath not touched it at all, dead though the house of it seems!" [1]

We distinguish arbitrarily between Spirit and Matter; but is there any distinction at root? That which is transitory, that which does change, that which belongs to 'time', is simply the *forms* which arise and disappear in this world as 'matter'; forms which range from Solar Systems and Universes to electrons and atoms in the physical world, and who knows what else in the superphysical?

[1] The *Song Celestial* (*Bhagavad Gita*), Sir Edwin Arnold.

How, then, about those forms which we know as mankind—ourselves ?

When we are told that " God created man in his own image ", we can accept the statement as literally true of Man's source and origin. But we can only do this if we de-materialise man, and regard him as a Cosmic Being, wholly and completely a spiritual Being in the first instance, and before his " fall into matter ". The statement is obviously and palpably untrue as regards physical man, or rather our *consciousness of man in the limitations of his physical nature.* We have seen that physical man was made " of the dust of the ground ", that his body evolved from what we commonly call ' dead ' matter. What possible likeness to God can we find in physical man at any of the stages of his physical evolution ? There was no individual physical man " in the beginning " of the Earth, of whom it could be said that he was " made in the image of God " ; neither did any such man dwell in a geographical Garden of Eden. All that has been talked about the locality of that ' Garden ' is pure nonsense. The four rivers and all the rest of the description are simply allegory.

We need not dwell here on the misrepresentations of the original meanings of the Hebrew words translated 'God' and 'Lord God', or of the perverted rendering of the sentences we have quoted. We may, for our present purpose, accept them as they stand.[1]

Man, as a spiritual or cosmic Being—if distinguishable as such from the Root Principle, or Principle-Substance—would at least be only one remove as it were from the Universal, and therefore quite clearly "made in the image of God" in so far as the word "made" can be said to be applicable at all.

Cosmic Man, like everything else in the universe that *exists* (*ex*, out, and *sisto*, to stand), must necessarily in a final analysis be identified with the One Root Principle, here called 'God'. But in so far as Man can be said to be distinguishable from the Universal—for example, just as physical matter is distinguishable as such from the Ether, though of the same substance—we can hardly conceive otherwise than that "in the beginning" he was so nearly akin to his Root and Source that the expression "made in the image of God" is quite a natural one.

[1] For more complete information on this question the reader may be referred to the work by Fabre d'Olivet, *La Langue Hebraique Restituée*, Paris, 1815. An English translation was published in 1921 by Putman, New York.

But we have this even more clearly set forth at the commencement of the Gnostic Gospel of St. John.

"In the beginning was the Word (Logos), and the Word was with God, and the Word was God. The same was in the beginning with God. All things were made by him; and without him was not anything made that hath been made. In him was life, and the life was the light of men."

As an alternative reading we have:

"All things were made through him; and without him was not anything made. That which hath been made was life in him; and the life was the light of men."

Identify this *Logos* with the archetypal Cosmic Man of Genesis, and the whole matter becomes as clear as day. Free it from all the obscurantism of theological dogma which identifies the Logos with the *personality* of Jesus of Nazareth, and at once we come into line with both science and philosophy.[1]

[1] The term *Logos* is pre-Christian. It stands for the concept of the divine thought or will uttering itself in objective form. Professor Max Müller in his work *Theosophy, or Psychological Religion*, tells us that, "*Logos* is a Greek word embodying a Greek thought, a thought which has its antecedents in Aristotle, in Plato; nay, the deepest roots of which have been traced back as far as the ancient philosophies of Anaxagoras and Heraclites" (p. 380). It is also embodied in the Sanscrit term *Vach*, speech, word in a mystical sense as the concrete expression of ideation.

How much the Gospels, and even St. Paul's Epistles, have been over-written to make them appear to support an already formulated theology we do not as yet know. Further scholarly researches, or the discovery of documents, may bring this more clearly into view. But the deeper interpretation which we are here putting forward is by no means new or unfamiliar to students; and it may clearly be seen even in the authorised version as it now stands.

Paul taught the doctrine of a Cosmic Christ *Principle*, which had to be "brought to birth" *in* each individual, even as it was manifested in the personality of Jesus of Nazareth.

But that Cosmic Christ, or Christ-Principle, we must identify with the Logos of St. John's Gospel; and the Logos of St. John's Gospel we must identify with the spiritual Cosmic Man of *Genesis*, "made in the image of God". But this Cosmic Man we must further identify with *ourselves*—when we have succeeded in de-individualising ourselves.

"All things (in this world of Man) were made by him." Of course. Man makes his own world. Man is the Creator of that world. It is all his own image-making (imagination), the *forms* in his " mind-stuff ". And by what is Man enlightened save by his own inner spiritual nature, the divine Cosmic Man, the Christos, the Anointed, " made in the image of God ", and, *as such*, still " eternal in the heavens."

> " In God, be sure, the soul in its highest prototype has never known creature, nor has she ever therein possessed time or space. For in this image (of God in the soul) everything is God : sour and sweet, good and bad, small and great, all are one in this image. This image is no more changed by anything in time than the divine nature is changed by anything that is creature : for it apprehends and uses all things according to the law of godhood " (Meister Eckhart).

Being thus in his original and prototypal aspect the Archetypal Divine Man, he is also the ' Saviour ' of the individual ' fallen ' man in whom he has to be " brought to birth ". But this bringing to birth of the " Christ in you " is the realisation by the individual of his inherent spiritual nature—which is precisely the definition of Religion which I have given as the basis of this work. The real man *is* the spiritual man ; and the realisation of this in the full consciousness of the *Christos* " in whom dwelleth all the fulness of the

Godhead bodily ", is the goal of his evolution.

Just as the divine Man, the Christos, is " one with the Father " as his Root and Source, so is the individual man one with 'Christ' as the divine Archetypal Man.

> " I am the vine, ye are the branches. As the branch cannot bear fruit of itself, except it abide in the vine ; so neither can ye, except ye abide in me " (John xv. 4, 5).

How clear this becomes when we transfer the conception from a personal historical Jesus, or 'Saviour', to that of the Cosmic Christ who is our own inner divine spiritual principle ; our real immortal Self, which knows neither birth nor death, and into the consciousness of which we must be re-generated—literally re-born—if we are to attain to " eternal life."

For how can these words apply in any sense to an individual personal historical 'Saviour'? They are literally true when we understand that our life, in all its aspects, even the life of each cell of our physical bodies, is " hid with Christ in God " (Col. iii. 3).

Life, the ONE LIFE, is eternal in its own nature, but not in the forms in which it manifests in time and space. These obviously all perish as such; therefore it is only as we learn to know ourselves apart from the temporary form, only as we learn to know ourselves as the Archetypal Man, "made in the image of God", that we can attain to that continuity of consciousness which alone can be spoken of as "life eternal". For verily we "fall asleep" out of that life when we incarnate; losing thereby all recollection of our previous existence and our eternal spiritual nature. Nor must we expect to do otherwise than incarnate again and again until this cycle of birth and death has been conquered through the attainment of a real spiritual consciousness, a cosmic consciousness, a Christ consciousness which transcends these alternate periods of sleeping and waking. "The last enemy that shall be abolished is death."

The true doctrine of immortality, of "eternal life", is not a doctrine of survival, or even of 'salvation', but of the immortal nature of the spiritual Ego in its own right and nature. It implies pre-existence as well as post-existence, for Spirit *is* the one eternal Root and Source of ALL.

This true doctrine was well understood in

the early centuries of the Christian era, and it was only in the sixth century, at the Second Council of Constantinople, A.D. 553, that the doctrine of reincarnation was made a heresy.

"Whosoever shall support the mythical doctrine of the pre-existence of the soul and the consequent wonderful opinion of its return, let him be anathema."

Can any rational person, with anything beyond the most limited parochial outlook on the Cosmic Process, conceive that Humanity as a whole has to pass through such a vast cycle of evolution, but that the individual only shares in that Process for the one brief flicker which is all that a single life-time represents in the millions of millions of years which comprise the whole Cycle?

The evolution of the individual must necessarily be commensurate with that of the Race: for how else does the Race progress save by the progression of the individual members thereof? What I may do in any one life-time not merely helps or hinders my own evolution, it helps or hinders also the evolution of the Race. The world of to-day is what the individuals of the past have made it; the world of to-morrow will be what the individuals of to-day are making it. That is denied by none. Is it to be supposed, then, that each generation as it springs up consists of souls who come from nowhere, who have had no past, but have to reap what previous generations have sown, and will have no share in reaping what they themselves are now sowing? Shall the law "what a man sows that shall he also reap" have no application here?

Nothing could be more irrational than to conceive that the individual *begins* when he is physically born—with more or less already developed faculties according to his fortunate, or unfortunate, parentage—and then forsooth goes on "for ever and ever", with no further share in the great evolutionary process. Nor is the matter improved by making a personal 'God' responsible for every soul that is born—one a savage, another a philosopher, a third a child of the slums, and yet a fourth a pampered child of fortune. There is either a great and inflexible law of justice (*Karma*) underlying all the varied attainments and circumstances of the individual, or else it is all the veriest chaos and caprice.

There is no space here, however, for a complete exposition of the teachings respecting reincarnation and karma; nor is the whole truth concerning these by any means available. It is both true and not true that 'I' reincarnate. What must be realised in the first instance is the distinction between the real immortal *Self* and the temporary conventional 'I'; between the *self* that must be 'lost' in order that the *Self* may be found. That higher *Self* is the *Christos*, the Christ *in* you.

The whole Cosmic Process is a perpetual reincarnation, and cycle within cycle the same principle obtains. The form perishes, but the *Life* is reborn in new forms. "All flesh"—all that pertains to the lower personal *self*—"is as grass"; and, slightly paraphrasing, we may say: "The grass withereth, and the flower falleth; but the *Self* abideth for ever."

The immortality or 'salvation' of the lower personal self is entirely dependent on its aspiration and union or at-one-ment with the higher spiritual Self, the *Christos*.

In the Genesis allegory, Adam is said to have fallen into a "deep sleep", whereby the physical separation of the sexes was brought about—to his still further 'fall' or undoing and loss of his spiritual nature, and even any recollection of it. And in this "deep sleep" the great majority of the Race exist to the present day. " But as in Adam all die, even so in Christos shall all be made alive again."

We must now examine the nature of this ' Fall ' somewhat more closely.

THE FALL OF MAN

ALTHOUGH in view of what has just been said, the 'salvation', or 'redemption', or 'regeneration' of the individual man, as well as of the whole Race, through a realisation of the original Divine Nature of Man, is perfectly clear and understandable, yet there is certainly an apparent difficulty here as regards the 'Fall'.

We have seen that we cannot accept the 'Fall' as being something which happened to "our first parents" considered as a single pair of physical individuals residing in a mythical Garden. What, then, does the allegory in *Genesis* mean; or rather, in what sense has Man fallen?

In the first place, and since the Archetypal Man is a *Cosmic* Being, the 'Fall' must certainly be a Cosmic Process. We must regard it as the outgoing of the unitary Cosmic Life, the ONE LIFE, into differentiation, or multiplicity—of form—or manifestation. We have a physical analogy in the formation out of the Cosmic Ether of the forms we know as physical matter; and we may very well conceive that the Cosmic Ether is still several removes from the One Root Principle.

The 'Fall', therefore, "in the beginning", is the outgoing from the ONE of some individualised Cosmic Life or Lives. In many ancient systems these were postulated to be the "Creative Gods": many different names being given to them, such as the *Prajâpatis* in the Eastern philosophy, or the *Sephiroth* of the *Kabbala*. In the New Testament we have seen it to be the *Logos*, and in Genesis it is Adam, the Archetypal Man "made in the image of God."

This first differentiation or outgoing is the commencement of the Cosmic Cyclic Process, or World-Process of evolution and involution; the evolution being the process of differentiation into more and more complex forms, the involution being the return to the Source or unity of the ONE, though this latter half of the cycle is usually termed evolution in so far as it relates to man's progress.

This return process is hardly as yet recognised in modern philosophy, though it is well recognised in the Eastern Scriptures, and is in fact, so far as the individual is concerned, the fundamental experience in all Mysticism, to whatever religion the mystic may belong.

In Eastern philosophy it is known as the outbreathing and inbreathing of Brahmâ; or sometimes as the Days and Nights of Brahmâ: the Days being the period of the whole cycle of objectivity, and the Nights the equally long period of subjectivity. Another term for these is Manvantara and Pralaya, and these major periods have minor periods or cycles of lesser duration, cycle within cycle.

Thus for the individual man the coming into incarnation is equivalent to a minor manvantara, or outgoing, and the time between any two incarnations is the equivalent pralaya or indrawing. A still lesser cycle is that of physical waking and sleeping.

So far as the great Cosmic Process as a whole is concerned, the why and wherefore of it is inscrutable. It has been the great problem ever since man began to think philosophically. Thus in the ancient *Rig Veda* we find the question asked:

> "Who knows the secret? who proclaimed it here?
> Whence, whence this manifold creation sprang?
> The Gods themselves came later into being—
> Who knows from whence this great creation sprang?
> That, whence all this great creation came,
> Whether Its will created or was mute,

The Most High Seer that is in highest heaven,
He knows it—or perchance even He knows not." [1]

In the fourteenth-century mystical Treatise, the *Theologia Germanica,* we find the question somewhat quaintly answered in this manner:

" If there ought not to be, and were not this and that—works, and a world full of real things, and the like—what were God Himself, and what had He to do, and whose God would He be ? "

But looking at the question from this cosmic point of view, the term 'Fall' is clearly inapplicable. We cannot say that God 'fell' when he willed to evolve the universe out of his own Substance—if indeed we can say that he *willed* at all.

" In this high consideration it is found that all is through and from God himself, and that it is his own substance, which is himself, and which he hath created out of himself " (Jacob Böhme, *The Three Principles of the Divine Essence,* Preface).

And if we cannot say that God 'fell', neither can we say that the Logos, the Archetypal Man, 'fell' when he, in his turn, had to

[1] Colebrook's trans.

repeat the act of creation, and evolve this world of his own.

The fact is that the term 'Fall' is only applicable when we regard the process from below, from the point of view of Humanity collectively—and also individually—in our already fallen condition as physical human beings. Then indeed we can say, " Oh, what a fall was (is) there ! "

And yet in some sense the 'Fall' must be *necessary*; a part of a divinely perfect WHOLE.

The Fall and Return are represented in the New Testament in the Parable of the Prodigal Son. The point is that in religion it is the Return which is the practical matter. Jacob Böhme postulates the Return as a universal law. " All things enter again into that whence they proceeded." [1]

Even physical science may be said to have recognised this to a certain extent in what is known as the law of entropy. Herbert Spencer, however, has stated it more clearly as follows :

" Apparently, the universally co-existent forces of attraction and repulsion, which, as we have seen, necessitate rhythm in all minor changes throughout

[1] *De Signatura Rerum*, XV, 42.

the universe also necessitate rhythm in the totality of its changes—produce now an immeasurable period during which the attracting forces predominating, cause universal concentration, and then an immeasurable period during which the repulsive forces predominating, cause universal diffusion—alternate eras of evolution and dissolution."

As regards the Logos, we have this principle stated by St. Paul in 1 Cor. xv. 28, as follows:

"When all things have been subjected unto him, then shall the son also himself be subjected to him that did subject all things unto him, that God may be all in all."

In other words, when the present cyclic process has run its course, so far as the Logos is concerned, then shall the Logos also be indrawn again into the ONE.

But this also is a concept which antedates St. Paul by many ages. In the Eastern Scriptures it is taught not merely that "the Gods themselves came later into being", but also that at the end of the Manvantara they and all else disappear—to reappear in the next Manvantara.

A free translation from the *Ordinances of Manu* might be given as follows:

"When the dissolution—Pralaya—had arrived at its term, The great Being—Param-Atma or Para-Purusha—the Lord existing through himself, out of whom and through whom all things were, and are and will be . . . resolved to emanate from his own substance the various creatures" (*Manava-Dharma-Sastra,* Book I, Slokas 6, 7).

"It is thus that, by an alternative waking and rest, the Immutable Beginning causes to revive and die eternally all the existing creatures, active and inert" (*Manu,* Book I, Sloka 50).

Now just as the ONE, or 'God', necessarily remains in his own nature and substance notwithstanding the creation, or emanation, or evolution of the Universe, so also does the Logos. The Logos creates his own particular world but yet *remains.* Here again we may take the analogy of Ether and physical matter. Physical matter is formed of the substance of the Ether, but yet the Ether *remains.* In the *Bhagavad Gita* we have Krishna, the Logos, saying: "I establish this whole world with a single portion of myself, and remain separate." [1]

[1] "Man in respect of his external comprehensible or finite body standeth only in a flitting figurative shadow or resemblance; and with his spiritual body he is the true essential *Word* of the divine property, in which God speaketh and begetteth His *Word*" (Jacob Böhme, *Epistles,* VI, 41).

So far as the individual man is concerned, his higher spiritual nature has often been referred to as the "divine spark". It is what Browning calls "the inmost centre in us all where truth abides in fulness." But, "wall upon wall, the gross flesh hems it in."

In the New Testament, as we have already seen, it is the "Christ in you", which must be "brought to birth." Man does not originate or grow that divine spark out of his physical nature in any sense whatsoever, biological or otherwise. On the contrary, it is that divine spark which grows him. It comes more and more into evidence as his evolution proceeds, and his physical organism is adapted to manifest it. The 'spark' at present burns dim in the great majority of the Race; and indeed, quite possibly, it may be "quenched" altogether in the individual. Then for that individual consciousness there is no 'salvation', no possibility of reuniting with his higher Self. The man "has a name that he lives", but is already spiritually dead, and for that *personality*, the lower self—which is merely a string of memories—there is nothing left but to fade out, even as a dream does. The spark has already been withdrawn, and there is no path by which the personal consciousness can follow.

This is quite clearly stated by Jesus in the Parable of the Vine.

> "If a man abide not in me [the Christos], he is cast forth as a branch, and is withered; and they gather them, and cast them into the fire, and they are burned" (John xv. 6).

This is certainly the fate of millions of the Race, so far as the *personality* is concerned. As regards the divine 'spark', that of course is immortal. It is not 'born' when it incarnates, neither does it 'die' when the body—or the 'person'—dies. It must seek another embodiment. I need hardly add that the 'fire' referred to in the text has nothing to do with the orthodox hell fire; though we cannot but believe that for the wicked man the process of annihilation of the personality after death is a long and desperate one. It is the "second death" referred to in *Revelation*.

But dimly as the spark burns in the great majority of the Race at the present stage of evolution, yet we have innumerable historical examples in which we see that it has been fanned into such a flame of divine Love that we cannot but regard these individuals as the highest and noblest of the Race. Moreover we are compelled to recognise that this quality of Life which we term *Love* must be in a transcendental degree the very essence and substance of the ONE LIFE in the fulness of its ineffable nature.

> "Pure and measureless love awakens joy within us; but love is a fathomless and soundless abyss; abyss calls to abyss; it is the Abyss of God calling the men of God. And this supreme invocation, this call out of the depths of the Abyss, which bids us come, appears to us as a shining dawn of essential light. It encompasses us and draws us, and we pass into the darkness, into the infinite darkness of God" (Ruysbroeck).

But though we cannot regard the Logos, the Christos, the Divine Man as having in any sense 'fallen', there is another aspect of the matter which is presented to us more specifically in the New Testament. It is the allegory of the Crucifixion. The Cross—the most ancient symbol in the world—signifies *matter*, the material universe. The Cosmic Process, the "descent of Spirit into Matter", is the crucifixion of the Divine Man in so far as that all the life and consciousness of every individual being—we might say of every individual atom—is part of his consciousness. It is all his 'body'. It is all one 'Vine', even as the branches are part of the Vine so long as they are not "withered and cast off". Yet even then there is a utility for the "withered branches" in Nature or the Cosmic Process. And herein lies the transcendental mystery of the sufferings of the Christ on the Cross "for the sins of the world." The sufferings of 'fallen' man, the sufferings of the world, "humanity's great pain", are the sufferings of the Divine Man.

We know that as the spark of divine Love becomes more and more in evidence in the individual, he feels more and more acutely the sufferings of his fellow creatures. This is because he becomes more and more identified with his own inner divine Principle, the *Christos*, and suffers—as represented in the Gospels and the allegory of the Crucifixion—for "the sins of the world." For verily the Divine Man is crucified in each one of us and in the whole Race. It is a present suffering, not a past historical event.

It is in each one of us also that Christ must "rise again from the dead." The Fall, the Incarnation, the Crucifixion, the Resurrection, are for the popular but ignorant Christianity of the Churches definite historical events; but for the mystic and the initiate they are perpetual cosmic and personal processes.

To what extent the personal Jesus of Nazareth accomplished these processes in his particular personality may best be left for each individual to decide for himself. At all events the historical Jesus as presented to us in the Gospels is almost universally recognised as the highest type of spiritual, or 'anointed', i.e. regenerated man, fully conscious of his divine nature and 'sonship'.

As for the allegory of the resurrection, we see from this that it has no reference whatever to a physical resurrection from an earthy tomb. It is the final victory of the individual over the deadness of his nature to spiritual realities. It is applicable either to the individual or to the Race as a whole. Thus we have the ringing cry of St. Paul: "*Awake, thou that sleepest, and arise from the dead, and Christ shall shine upon thee*" (Eph. v. 14).

The whole context of this verse shows that this applies to the living, not to the dead in their graves. It is the meaning which attaches to 'death' all through the New

Testament, though it is so often made to appear as if it referred to physical death. And who so fearful of physical death as the orthodox Christian? It is this materialised 'Christianity' more than anything else that has 'put the fear of death' into the minds of so many millions—and then taught that they could be 'saved' by priestly intervention or profession of 'faith' in man-made doctrines.

"The fear of death does not manifest itself or develop in the great religions until the latter begin to be corrupted for the benefit of priests and kings. The intuition and intelligence of mankind have never again reached the height which they attained when they conceived the ideal of divinity of which we find the most authentic traces in the Vedic traditions. One might say that, in those days man disclosed, at the topmost height of his stature, and thus established, once for all, that conception of the divine which he subsequently forgot and frequently degraded; but despite oblivion and ephemeral pervertion, its light was never lost" (M. Maeterlinck, *The Great Secret*, p. 135).

This is but a brief outline of the great history of Man in his Cosmic as well as his individual aspects; mainly as presented in the Scripture of the West.

So-called 'Christianity' has arrogated to itself a superiority over all preceding teachings, and has claimed for itself a 'revelation' in the person of Jesus of Nazareth of facts as to Man's spiritual condition and nature which were previously unknown.

This claim cannot be sustained in the light of our modern knowledge of ancient teachings and ancient Scriptures. The real fact is that every one of its teachings is derived from earlier sources, and the allegories and myths which appear in the Jewish Scriptures and in the New Testament were current ages before these were written. But these teachings have to be repeated over and over again, now in one form, now in another; for the fate of all such *mystical* teachings, of truths which can only be presented in the form of allegory or myth, is always and ever to be materialised and literalised. Such, indeed, has been the fate of the teachings re-presented once more by certain Initiates in the Christian Scriptures. Many writers have tried, and are trying to-day, to bring the inner spiritual meaning to the understanding of the more intelligent minds of the community; but the Church with its 'orthodoxy' still stands in the way. It must, in fact stultify its whole history and teaching if it now abandons the literal interpretation of the Scriptures on which it has built its theology and claims. Still, in the end, the Truth must prevail.

So soon as we have recognised that the *Christos* is a universal cosmic *principle*—the "light which lighteth every man coming into the world"—quite distinct from any particular historical character in whom this *principle* may have been manifested in a supreme degree: it matters not whether we call it Christos, or Krishna, or Horus, or Osiris, or by the name of any other 'heathen' god, the traditional 'events' in whose life have been reproduced more or less closely in the Gospel narratives—for example, virgin birth, crucifixion, resurrection, etc.[1]—each and every 'religion' may then find this *principle* as the true inner spiritual basis of its scriptures and traditions, subsequently materialised, literalised, and in general secularised for the benefit of a priestly caste.

We may conclude by examining very briefly some aspects of the ancient *Gnôsis* teachings as to Man's individual nature and Cosmic relations and origin.

[1] *Cf.* Doane's *Bible Myths.*

The Ancient Gnôsis

We have already shown by a few quotations from ancient sources how the very deepest spiritual truths have been apprehended and stated from the remotest times. In some cases they have been stated quite plainly; in others they have been embodied in allegory and myth. There is every evidence to show that there has always existed a real *Gnôsis* concerning the deeper aspects of the universe and of Man's nature: a Gnôsis which has always had its Initiates, Masters, Adepts, and Hierophants. It was they who framed the allegories and symbols, who wrote the Scriptures of the world, who built the Great Pyramid, and in other ways made manifest this Ancient Wisdom.

To suppose that all the pre-Christian nations were without any real spiritual knowledge or truth, or only had a dim light to guide them, is one of those conceits of 'Christianity' which appears so detestable to the well informed to-day. It might perhaps have been excused some fifty or sixty years ago when practically nothing was known of

Eastern religions and philosophy; it cannot be held to-day for one moment by anyone who has made any study at all of comparative religion and philosophy.

In the far back ages, millenniums before the Christian era—how many we do not know—the ancient Seers and Initiates had already arrived at the conception of One Eternal Immutable PRINCIPLE which IS the Universe in its wholeness. And they had already arrived at the conception that the individuality of the individual was a mere appearance; that in reality there was nothing separate from the ONE; and they had expressed this in the now well-known aphorism of the *Upanishads*, THAT ART THOU.

> "What that subtle Being is, of which this whole Universe is composed, that is the Real, that is the Soul, *That art thou*, O Svetaketa" (*Chandogya Upanishad*, VI, 14, 3).

> "Verily he who has seen, heard, comprehended and known the Self, by him is this entire universe known" (*Brihad-aranyaka Upanishad*, II, 4, 5).

"As the flowing rivers in the ocean
Disappear, quitting name and form,
So the knower, being liberated from name and form,

Goes unto the heavenly Person, higher than the high."

Mundaka Upanishad, III, 2, 8.

The following extracts from Professor Max Müller's work, *Theosophy or Psychological Religion,* are a commentary on these quotations.

" We must remember that the fundamental principle of the Vedanta-philosophy was not ' Thou are *He* ', but Thou art *That,* and it was not Thou *wilt be,* but Thou *art.* This ' Thou art ' expresses something that is, that has been, and always will be, not something that has still to be achieved, or is to follow, for instance, after death. . . . By true knowledge the individual soul does not *become* Brahman, but *is* Brahman, as soon as it knows what it really is, and always has been." (p. 284).

" This is the gist of what I call *Psychological Religion,* or Theosophy, the highest summit of thought which the human mind has reached, which has found different expressions in different religions and philosophies, but nowhere such a clear and powerful realisation as in the ancient Upanishads of India." (p. 105).

So also the old Chinese philosopher Chuang Tzu :

" He who knows what God is, and who knows what Man is, has attained. Knowing what God is, he knows that he himself proceeded therefrom."

To-day the Western world is attaining to a knowledge of this deeper Gnôsis from many different directions: through archeological discoveries, through scholarly researches, through the revival of Theosophy in the Theosophical Movement initiated in 1875 by Mme. H. P. Blavatsky, and through the writings of our modern mystics, seers, and transcendentalists.

The following quotation from *The Great Secret*, by M. Maeterlinck, may be given as representative of the views of many writers and thinkers to-day. It is also worth quoting in view of what we have already put forward as regards biological evolution, and the present subject of the ancient Gnôsis.

" 'When this world had emerged from darkness,' says the *Bhagavata Purana*, which according to the Hindus is contemporary with the *Veda*, 'the subtile elementary principle produced the vegetable seed which first of all gave life to the plants. From the plants life passed into the fantastic creatures which were born of the slime in the waters; then, through a series of different shapes and animals, it came to man.' . . . 'They passed in succession by way of the plants, the worms, the insects, the serpents, the tortoises, cattle and the wild animals—such is the lower stage,' says Manu again, who adds: 'Creatures acquired the qualities of those that preceded them, so that the farther down its position in the series, the greater its qualities.'

"Have we not here the whole of the Darwinian evolution confirmed by geology and foreseen at least six thousand years ago? One might give an infinite number of these disquieting examples. Whence did our prehistoric ancestors, in their supposed terrible state of ignorance and abandonment, derive those extraordinary intuitions, that knowledge and assurance which we ourselves are scarcely reconquering? And if their ideas were correct upon certain points which we are able by chance to verify, have we not reason to ask ourselves whether they may not have seen matters more correctly and further ahead than we did in respect of many other problems, as to which they are equally definite in their assertions but which have hitherto been beyond our verification? One thing is certain, that to reach the stage at which they then stood they must have had behind them a treasury of traditions, observations, and experiences—in a word, of wisdom—of which we find it difficult to form any conception; but in which, while waiting for something better, we ought to place rather more confidence than we have done, and by which we might well benefit, assuaging our fears and learning to understand and reassure ourselves in respect of our future beyond the tomb, and guiding our lives." (p. 43).

Thus Christianity in its traditional form has not merely nothing new to tell us, but is a sad materialisation and limitation of the ancient Gnôsis of which it should have been a restatement. Even the Christian mystics are only repeating the experiences of the mystics and seers of all time. How could it be otherwise? Their experiences, where valid, and not mere self-induced visions, must necessarily correspond, and they one and all testify to the one fundamental fact, *the oneness of the individual and the Universal.*

Let us examine a few rather more modern statements.

> "Am I not with God's Godhead
> essentially one?
> How else is He my Father? how else am I
> His Son.
>
> "Spark from the Fire! Drop from the Sea!
> O man, what art thou then
> Unless to thine Eternal Source
> Thou dost return again?"
>
> —Angelus Silesius.

"When the will is so united that it becometh a One in oneness, then doth the Heavenly Father produce his only-begotten Son in Himself and in me. Wherefore in Himself and in me? I am one with Him—He cannot exclude me. In the self-same operation doth the Holy Ghost receive his existence, and proceeds from me as from God. Wherefore?

I am in God, and if the Holy Ghost deriveth not his being from me, He deriveth it not from God. I am in nowise excluded.

"God in himself was not God—in the creature only hath He become God. I ask to be rid of God—that is, that God, by his grace, would bring me into the Essence—that Essence which is above God and above distinction. I would enter into that eternal Unity which was mine before all time, when I was what I would, and would what I was:—into a state above all addition or diminution;—into the Immobility whereby all is moved" (Meister Eckhart).

"St. John says: 'All things were made by Him,' that means *one* life in Him. That which man was in himself when created, that he was eternally in God. As long as a man does not attain to the purity with which he came forth, when first created out of nothing, he will never truly come to God" (John Tauler).

"All whatsoever it is that liveth and moveth is in God, and *God himself is all*, and whatsoever is formed or framed, is formed *out of* Him, be it either out of love or out of wrath" (Jacob Böhme).

"God giveth power to every life, be it good or bad, unto each thing, according to its desire, for He Himself is All; and yet He is not called God according to every being, but according to the light wherewith He dwelleth in Himself, and shineth with His power through all His beings. He giveth in His power to all His beings and works, and each thing receiveth His power according to its property; one taketh darkness, the other light; each hunger desireth its property, and yet the whole essence or being is all God's, be it evil or good, for from Him and through Him are all things; what is not His love, that is His anger." (Jacob Böhme).

"Men possess virtues and the Divine likeness in differing measure; in greater or lesser degree have they found their essence in the depths of themselves, according to their dignity. But God fulfils all; and each, clearer or fainter, according to the measure of his love, possesses the sense of God's presence in the depths of his own being." (Ruysbroeck).

CONCLUSION

OUR conclusion, then, is simply this: The Religion of the Future will be no new thing; it will be a clear understanding and appreciation of what has been taught by Mystics, Seers, and Initiates in all ages of which we have any literary records—and probably ages before that. Its fundamental principle has never been better realised or stated than in the ancient *Upanishads*: more particularly in that single aphorism, THAT ART THOU.

At every point of his nature and existence—whether as a physical being, or in the powers of his mind, or, deeper still, in the innermost root and source of his life and consciousness—the individual touches the universal, and derives all his substance and his powers therefrom. The more he de-individualises himself, the more will his consciousness expand towards the universal. Hence it is precisely his present sense of separateness which is the great illusion, the great heresy, the great 'Fall': and so the cause of all that we call *Evil*. Man has not merely separated himself in consciousness from 'God', but even from any sense of unity with his fellow man—let alone the 'lower orders of creation' with whom he is physically akin. It is nothing but this individualism and self-seeking which is the cause of all the bitter strife and conflict in the world; from that of one religion with another to the sordid struggle for existence in our so-called 'civilized' communities.

Religion in its proper understanding is the *return* of Man to consciousness of his divine or spiritual nature and powers.

> "As in Adam all die (to the consciousness of their spiritual nature) even so in Christ (the divine spark within) shall all be made alive again" (to that consciousness).

Thus Religion is *a quality of life,* not a mere belief or profession of 'faith'. Religion in its exoteric or doctrinal form must first of all bring this fundamental principle to the *intellectual* apprehension of mankind in general. Instead of setting one religion against another, and endeavouring simply to proselytise, it must endeavour to find the points of contact and similarity. Individual religion merely ministers to and aggravates the evils of separateness—of which we have no better example than in the history of ecclesiastical Christianity.

How far the religion of the future can be institutional and yet avoid the fearful evils which have so far attached to institutional religions, is a problem which can only be worked out gradually; but it is the clearest of the clear that there can be no possible intermediary between the individual and his own inner divine Self. Each individual must "work out his own salvation" in his own inner experience. No one can possibly do that for him. The deep quality of *faith* in his own inner nature and powers will supply the right motive and the right will to press forward to an ever-increasing *realisation*. The life of the spirit that is *lived*—that is the only true religion, let the individual profess what doctrines he may. But the *life* is above all doctrines.

We apprehend, therefore, that so far as religion in the future may be institutional it will have no resemblance to the present methods and claims of any priestly hierarchy. It may be instructional—yes; but the instructors will be those who *know*, not an ignorant priesthood who may even be "weak-minded and depraved in habits",[1] and yet not merely supposed to be capable of instructing the people but also of administering a "sacred office".

[1] *Catholicism*, by the Rev. M. C. D'Arcy, S.J., p. 31.

There will be no "places of worship"; for these belong to the primitive ideas of Deity, the anthropomorphic conception of a personal God who requires acknowledgment of his sovereign power; who requires adoration, subserviency, honour, ritual, court etiquette, and what not, exactly as earthly Potentates used to do—only more so. In actual practice the 'honours' appear to have gone rather to the Hierarchy than to the Deity.

What will the individual, what will the Race become, when "the earth shall be full of (this) knowledge of the LORD as the waters cover the sea"? (Isaiah xi. 9).

"Such a man, as Adam was before his Eve (before he fell into generation) shall arise and again enter into, and eternally possess Paradise." (Jacob Böhme, *Mysterium Magnum*, XVIII, 3).

That is the necessary and inevitable end of Man's great Pilgrimage. The return is as certain as the 'Fall'; but the why and wherefore of the Pilgrimage we have yet to learn.

"The Most High Seer that is in highest heaven,
He knows it—or perchance even he knows not."

But the great and practical point *now* is,

that the individual need not wait for the slow progress of the Race. There are to-day, as of old, Initiates, Adepts, Masters of the Divine Science of the Soul, waiting to take the individual in hand as soon as he is ready to take the next forward step. And so surely as the individual seeks to do this, so surely shall he find ; and it is only those who do seek who find—exactly what they seek and in the form in which they seek it. The mind moulds its own forms. Seek therefore only that which is formless.

The supreme Truth is formless—or rather it is embodied in all forms. But this can only be apprehended as the individual frees himself from form.

Even so must the religion of the future be free from forms and formulas, and yet make use of these for precisely what they can serve towards an appreciation of the one central Truth.

When we have apprehended that Central Truth we are above the innumerable forms of religion in which the Race at various times has endeavoured to grope after this truth, and at other times has perverted it. Then we can speak to the Christian as a Christian, and to the Buddhist as a Buddhist, and to each and every one in his own language, and in the measure of his capacity to understand.

What the great Neoplatonist and Hermetic philosopher, Jamblichus, wrote, about the year A.D. 300, will serve to show once more that there were in those times those who *knew* ; nor can we suppose that this knowledge has ever been lost to the world. It was only lost through the dark ages of the dominance of the Christian Hierarchy. With this Hierarchy the *Gnôsis* became a heresy, and the seekers after the deeper knowledge were burnt at the stake, whilst the masses became sunk in ignorant superstitions. But there always remained a Hierarchy of Initiates, withdrawn from the world, who, as Philo tells us :

> "Such men, though few in number, keep alive the covered spark of Wisdom secretly, throughout the cities (of the world), in order that virtue may not be absolutely quenched and vanish from our human kind."

Here then is what Jamblichus tells us :

> "But there is another principle of the soul, which is superior to all nature and generation, and through which we are capable of being united to the Gods, of transcending the mundane order, and of participating eternal life, and the energy of the supercelestial Gods. Through this principle, therefore,

we are able to liberate ourselves from fate. For when the more exalted parts of us energise, and the soul is elevated to natures better than itself, then it is entirely separated from things which detain it in generation, departs from subordinate natures, exchanges the present for another life, and gives itself to another order of things, entirely abandoning the former order with which it was connected."

Also Plotinus:

"This, therefore, is the life of the Gods, and of divine and happy men, a liberation from all terrene concerns, a life unaccompanied with human pleasures and a flight of the alone to the alone." (Enn. vi, 9, 11).

Is this in any way different from the 'Gospel' of St. Paul?

"But we all, with unveiled face (or rather mind) reflecting as in a mirror the glory of the Lord (the Spirit), are transformed into the same image from glory to glory" (2 Cor. iii. 18).

And from a priceless little modern mystical treatise, *Light on the Path*:

"Seek the way by making the profound obeisance of the soul to the dim star that burns within. Steadily, as you watch and worship, its light will grow stronger. Then you may know that you have found the beginning of the way. And when you have found the end its light will suddenly become the infinite light."

When all men, all the Race of Mankind—every individual now struggling on the upward path, the return journey, through incarnation after incarnation—shall thus have realised, individually and collectively, their divine spiritual nature: then, and then only, shall be fulfilled the prophecy of the "second coming":

> "The kingdom of the world is become the kingdom of our Lord, and of his Christ: and he shall reign unto the ages of the ages" (Rev. xi. 15).

But in the meanwhile the "second coming" is also an individual achievement. It is achieved *in* each individual who has reached the end of his great pilgrimage, and for whom the 'divine spark', the "Christ *in* you", has become "the infinite light".

And the teaching is the same whether we take it in terms of Buddhism or of the Christian Scriptures.[1]

The goal, the consummation is the same whether we speak of the individual as having "achieved Nirvana", or as having been "made alive again in Christ".

[1] I cannot say "Christianity," because Ecclesiastical Christianity does not teach this, nor does it recognise that the fundamental truths of Buddhism are the same as those of the Christian Scriptures.

"As one who stands on yonder snowy horn
Having nought o'er him but the boundless blue,
So, these sins being slain, the man is come
Nirvana's verge unto.

Him the Gods envy from their lower seats;
Him the Three Worlds in ruin should not shake;
All life is lived for him, all deaths are dead;
Karma will no more make

New houses. Seeking nothing, he gains all;
Foregoing self, the Universe grows 'I'."

—*Light of Asia.*

Or, again, in the words of the Christian Scriptures:

"He that overcometh, I will make him a pillar in the temple of my God, and he shall go out thence (into incarnation) no more." (Rev. iii. 12).

That 'temple' is Man himself—Cosmic Man, "eternal in the heavens." "Know ye not that ye are the temple of God." (1 Cor. iii. 16).

This fundamental fact of *the divine nature of Man* as the *Christos* is what I apprehend must be taught as *The Religion of the Future.*

Through the long, long evolutionary Cosmic Process the divine spark or 'Monad' passes through the lower kingdoms of Nature until it reaches the animal and the human, where it begins to appear as a *self-conscious* activity.

Through the long, long evolutionary history of the Race the self-conscious individual gradually, and by many a bitter experience, learns to transcend his animal nature: in the first place by the cultivation of *intellect* or the higher powers of Mind, but ultimately by 'bringing to birth' the powers of *Spirit*. Hence arise, from feeble beginnings the innumerable forms of 'religion'.

But let it not be thought that any mere conformity to a particular religion, or 'belief' in any specific doctrines, is the end of the struggle, the attainment of the goal. Much less can it be thought that it is a mere question of being 'saved' in the sense of going to heaven 'for ever and ever'. The individual who has really *attained*, who has become *Christos*, who has reached the goal of the present evolutionary cycle of Humanity, possesses a Cosmic Consciousness and Cosmic Powers the very possibility of which would be commonly denied by the great majority. Nor would it be fitting that the world at large should realise the possibility of the possession of these powers by each individual; for until the quality of *divine compassion* has been correspondingly developed, they may be used for selfish ends—with dire disaster both for the individual and the Race. Hence the possessors of these powers must remain unknown to the world in general, though not so to those whose qualifications entitle them to recognition and instruction by them.

"The last enemy that shall be abolished is death."

The individual who has really *attained* has conquered this "last enemy," both in the physical and in the spiritual sense.

In the spiritual sense we have already seen that 'death' means deadness to our own inherent spiritual nature. In the physical sense its conquest means the end of the great cycle of physical births and deaths, or reincarnations—or, as it is called in the Eastern Scriptures, *sangsāra*, the continual round of births and deaths.

"Karma will no more make new houses."

And so the individual who has *attained* takes a physical body or not of his own will and design for the helping of Humanity, out of his sensitiveness to "humanity's great pain," and not because *Karma* forces him to do so. The Eastern Scriptures and the Western Scriptures teach fundamentally the same truths as to man's nature and destiny.

What else the man who has attained, who is *Christos*, *is* and *does*, cannot be set down here; nor can any but his fellow initiates know or even conceive of that divine glory which yet is everyone's birthright.

> " He standeth now like a white pillar to the west, upon whose face the rising Sun of thought eternal poureth forth its first most glorious waves. His mind, like a becalmed and boundless ocean, spreadeth out in shoreless space. He holdeth life and death in his strong hand.
>
> " Yea, He is mighty. The living power made free in him, that power which is HIMSELF, can raise the tabernacle of illusion high above the gods, above great Brahm and Indra.
>
> " Hark ! . . . from the deep unfathomable vortex of that golden light in which the Victor bathes, ALL NATURE'S wordless voice in thousand tones ariseth to proclaim :
>
> " JOY UNTO YE, O MEN.
>
> " A PILGRIM HATH RETURNED BACK 'FROM THE OTHER SHORE.'
>
> " A NEW ARHAN IS BORN."

Even so may all who read this be " born again " into the " golden light " of the Divine *Christos*.

INDEX

ORDER FROM YOUR FAVORITE BOOKSELLER OR CALL FOR OUR FREE CATALOG

Of Heaven and Earth: Essays Presented at the First Sitchin Studies Day, edited by Zecharia Sitchin. ISBN 1-885395-17-5 • 164 pages • 5 1/2 x 8 1/2 • trade paper • illustrated • $14.95

God Games: What Do You Do Forever?, by Neil Freer. ISBN 1-885395-39-6 • 312 pages • 6 x 9 • trade paper • $19.95

Space Travelers and the Genesis of the Human Form: Evidence of Intelligent Contact in the Solar System, by Joan d'Arc. ISBN 1-58509-127-8 • 208 pages • 6 x 9 • trade paper • illustrated • $18.95

Humanity's Extraterrestrial Origins: ET Influences on Humankind's Biological and Cultural Evolution, by Dr. Arthur David Horn with Lynette Mallory-Horn. ISBN 3-931652-31-9 • 373 pages • 6 x 9 • trade paper • $17.00

Past Shock: The Origin of Religion and Its Impact on the Human Soul, by Jack Barranger. ISBN 1-885395-08-6 • 126 pages • 6 x 9 • trade paper • illustrated • $12.95

Flying Serpents and Dragons: The Story of Mankind's Reptilian Past, by R.A. Boulay. ISBN 1-885395-38-8 • 276 pages • 6 x 9 • trade paper • illustrated • $19.95

Triumph of the Human Spirit: The Greatest Achievements of the Human Soul and How Its Power Can Change Your Life, by Paul Tice. ISBN 1-885395-57-4 • 295 pages • 6 x 9 • trade paper • illustrated • $19.95

Mysteries Explored: The Search for Human Origins, UFOs, and Religious Beginnings, by Jack Barranger and Paul Tice. ISBN 1-58509-101-4 • 104 pages • 6 x 9 • trade paper • $12.95

Mushrooms and Mankind: The Impact of Mushrooms on Human Consciousness and Religion, by James Arthur. ISBN 1-58509-151-0 • 103 pages • 6 x 9 • trade paper • $12.95

Vril or Vital Magnetism, with an Introduction by Paul Tice. ISBN 1-58509-030-1 • 124 pages • 5 1/2 x 8 1/2 • trade paper • $12.95

The Odic Force: Letters on Od and Magnetism, by Karl von Reichenbach. ISBN 1-58509-001-8 • 192 pages • 6 x 9 • trade paper • $15.95

The New Revelation: The Coming of a New Spiritual Paradigm, by Arthur Conan Doyle. ISBN 1-58509-220-7 • 124 pages • 6 x 9 • trade paper • $12.95

The Astral World: Its Scenes, Dwellers, and Phenomena, by Swami Panchadasi. ISBN 1-58509-071-9 • 104 pages • 6 x 9 • trade paper • $11.95

Reason and Belief: The Impact of Scientific Discovery on Religious and Spiritual Faith, by Sir Oliver Lodge. ISBN 1-58509-226-6 • 180 pages • 6 x 9 • trade paper • $17.95

William Blake: A Biography, by Basil De Selincourt. ISBN 1-58509-225-8 • 384 pages • 6 x 9 • trade paper • $28.95

The Divine Pymander: And Other Writings of Hermes Trismegistus, translated by John D. Chambers. ISBN 1-58509-046-8 • 196 pages • 6 x 9 • trade paper • $16.95

Theosophy and The Secret Doctrine, by Harriet L. Henderson. Includes ***H.P. Blavatsky: An Outline of Her Life,*** by Herbert Whyte, ISBN 1-58509-075-1 • 132 pages • 6 x 9 • trade paper • $13.95

www.ingramcontent.com/pod-product-compliance
Lightning Source LLC
LaVergne TN
LVHW020637100826
845148LV00012B/2218
* 9 7 8 1 5 8 5 0 9 3 2 5 0 *